From Ashes to Life

From Ashes to Life
My Memories of the Holocaust

Lucille Eichengreen

with Harriet Hyman Chamberlain

MERCURY HOUSE
San Francisco, California

Author's note: This book is based on my remembrances. The individuals mentioned were real; in some cases, the names have been changed. I have attempted to stay as close as possible to the truth of my experiences. Historical events are accurate. However, remembrances do not allow for similar certainty. Therefore, there may be some minor discrepancies in the interpretations of the events or the dates of their occurrence.

Published in the United States by
Mercury House
San Francisco, California

United States Constitution, First Amendment: Congress shall make no law respecting an establishment of religion, or prohibiting the free exercise thereof; or abridging the freedom of speech, or of the press; or the right of the people peaceably to assemble, and to petition the Government for a redress of grievances.

Mercury House and colophon are registered trademarks
of Mercury House, Incorporated

Photos courtesy of Lucille Eichengreen
Printed on acid-free paper
Manufactured in the United States of America

Library of Congress Cataloging-in-Publication Data
Eichengreen, Lucille, 1925–
    From ashes to life: my memories of the Holocaust / Lucille Eichengreen with Harriet Hyman Chamberlain.
        p.   cm.
    ISBN 1–56279–052–8
    1. Holocaust, Jewish (1939–1945)—Personal narratives.   2. Eichengreen, Lucille, 1925– .   I. Chamberlain, Harriet Hyman, 1929– .
II. Title.
D804.3.E43   1994
940.53'18—dc20   93–12727
                                                                CIP

5   4   3   2

For Dan, Barry, and Martin ⁓

Contents ∼

Acknowledgments ～

My deep gratitude and thanks go to my many friends and family, without whose help and support this book would not have been possible. Primarily, I want to thank Harriet Hyman Chamberlain, who listened with endless and unselfish patience and who worked with me in all phases of the writing and rewriting of my remembrances. Jack Chamberlain gave freely of his compassion and understanding. I owe a debt of special thanks to Lucjan Dobroszycki for his thoughtful suggestions and historical and editorial comments. Harriet Renaud read and commented on my many drafts. Sheldon Rothblatt offered valuable ideas and empathy. My close friend, the late Malka Heifetz Tussman, was most influential in initiating my writing of this book.

I am grateful to Mercury House and Tom Christensen, David Peattie, Barbara Stevenson, Ellen Towell, Sarah Malarkey, Hazel White, Nancy Palmer Jones, Timothy Gable, and Zipporah Collins for producing this book with great care and attention to my concerns. And last but certainly not least, my unending gratitude to my husband, Dan, and our sons, Barry and Martin, for their support, encouragement, and love.

The parchment burns—the letters soar upward.

— Talmud

Foreboding ∾

1933–1938

> *The sun stopped shining—*
> *Insignificant, small,*
> *Young, and innocent,*
> *I stopped my carefree play.*
> *Bright colors hurt my eyes,*
> *the sky turned gray*
> *and remained dull and threatening.*
> *Whispers surrounded me,*
> *and my world turned upside down.*
> *Suddenly I was a child outcast—*
> *Why?*
> *Failing to understand, I smiled*
> *as fear gripped my throat.*
> *Fear of what? I asked.*
> *But found no answer.*

*F*ather was bending over my bed kissing my cheek.

"It's time to get up, Celia. Today we must pack and start our trip home."

"Finally," I sighed with relief.

I had missed our usual summer trip from our home in Hamburg, Germany, to visit Mother's large family in Sambor, Poland. This year, we had spent the entire summer in Bad Schwartau so that I could recuperate, taking baths and medications to cure a severe throat infection that had kept me bedridden for most of the past winter. We had arrived early in June, and now it was already August. It had been a long three months.

The spa was located not far from Lübeck and was frequented mostly by elderly people. I hated it. My sister Karin had sat at my bedside all through the summer to keep me company when I was supposed to rest. But a happy three-year-old, five years younger than I, was not enough company for me. The one good thing that had happened during our stay in Bad Schwartau was that boredom had led me to read everything that had come into my hands. Now, however, I was impatient to get home, to see my friends, and to resume school.

I sat up in bed and smiled at my father. "If I put all my things on the bed, will you and Mother put them into suitcases for me?" I asked.

Father nodded. He seemed pleased; he knew how much I wanted to go home. By early afternoon all the suitcases were packed and stood ready in the hall.

"Finished," Father said. "Let's go one last time into the garden to have tea and say our good-byes to Mr. Becker, who was so kind to rent this house to us for the summer."

Mother, who had come in dressed in her blue linen traveling suit, nodded. Karin and I combed our hair, washed our hands, and walked downstairs.

Mr. Becker was the owner and manager of the estate with its gardens and stables. He also raised horses, and once he had noticed my interest in them, he occasionally permitted me to ride an especially docile brown mare. He was kind and gentle with his horses and patient with me as he explained how to use the saddle, how to pull the reins and use the stirrups. He was a short, stout, unusually jolly man, with a red face, blue eyes, and sparse, stringy blond hair. He seemed to like me and expressed his feelings by frequently pinching my face. I hated the touch of his fingers on my skin, but I dared not complain. Today, however, I didn't mind going to the formal afternoon get-together at Mr. Becker's coffee table in the garden. After all, I thought, tomorrow I will be home.

The round table stood under a willow tree. It was covered with a pink tablecloth and set with flowery china. In the center sat a round plate with strawberry tarts. The sun was bright, the wind warm, and I was happy.

Mr. Becker was seated at the table waiting for us. He rose as we approached and invited us to sit down. Eager and smiling, his ruddy face redder than usual, he sputtered with pleasure. As he pinched my cheek, I winced and looked at him as if seeing him for the first time. His neck almost disappeared inside his shirt, and his tie seemed to be choking him. His jacket was too tight, his forehead was wet with perspiration, his stringy hair was in disarray, and his blue eyes were bulging. He looked uncomfortable. He also smelled of beer. He was an unpleasant sight and smell by any standard but especially to an eight-year-old.

"Thank you for letting us rent a house and stay here these past three months," my father began.

"Well, Mr. Landau, I hope you and your family enjoyed your stay and that you will return next year." Mr. Becker was obviously feeling talkative.

"Yes, we'll think about it. For now, we're packed and will be leaving shortly," my father replied.

Mr. Becker just nodded. He seemed eager to talk about

something else that was on his mind. "Mr. Landau," he said, "have you noticed how, since Hitler came to power earlier this year, the mood in Germany has changed for the better?"

There was complete silence. Mr. Becker had asked a question, but Father didn't seem to hear, nor did he respond.

In spite of this, Mr. Becker plunged on: "Economic conditions are on the upswing, unemployment is dwindling, our social benefits have increased, and last but not least, Hitler will take care of the Jews!"

Once again there was silence, except for the sound of our breathing. Then my father stood up abruptly and gripped the edges of the table, his knuckles turning white.

"Mr. Becker," Father said in a steady but cold voice, "I am a Jew. We are Jews." His angry voice frightened me, and I wondered what this was all about.

A speechless and embarrassed Mr. Becker fumbled for words while his face turned even redder. "Well . . . ," he sputtered, "I didn't mean you, of course. I'm talking about the other Jews—you're not like them . . ."

My father didn't give him a chance to finish. He took my hand and Karin's and nodded to Mother. He hurried us out of the garden, collected our bags, and almost immediately had a taxi waiting to take us to the train station.

Later, on the train to Hamburg, I heard Father and Mother use a word that was new to me: *antisemitism.*

"What does that word mean?" I wanted to know.

"What word?" Father asked.

"Antisemitism," I replied.

Father's answer was short, almost abrupt. "Only stupid people are antisemitic. They hate Jews without reason."

I still did not understand, but Father had turned away to

read his paper, signaling that he was no longer willing to talk. I was confused. I knew we were Jews, that we observed religious customs, that I attended a private Jewish school. There was certainly some connection, but what did this hatred have to do with us? I wanted to ask more questions and get more answers. I moved closer, tugging at Father's sleeve.

Finally, he reacted. "Please, read your book," he pleaded. "You're too young to understand, and I've told you all you need to know."

I had never seen Father this upset. Obviously antisemitism was bad. But why? And what did it mean that Hitler would "take care of the Jews"?

"Please talk to me," I begged.

Father kissed the top of my head. "Someday," he said, "when you are old enough to understand."

A few moments later, Mother leaned over and put her arms around me. "Now that Karin is asleep," she said softly, "I'll tell you what I remember about antisemitism. You know I grew up in Sambor with four older brothers and three sisters. I was about your age, maybe a little younger, when I heard the neighbors shouting through the open door, 'Another pogrom, quick, hide the young girls!'"

"What is a pogrom?" I asked.

"Well, a pogrom is when a group of people get together and do hateful things to Jews. They break up homes, burn them, and hurt innocent people. My brothers and sisters knew what the pogrom warning meant. It had happened before, and they remembered. But I was too young to remember. Anyway, my mother grabbed me, told me to be very, very quiet, and pushed me inside the huge kitchen stove. I waited there a long, long time, until finally I was taken out and told that the pogromniks had left."

"But who are the pogromniks—who are the people who did this?" I asked.

"They are bad people, often soldiers, sometimes peasants, who hate and kill Jews. This hate is called antisemitism."

I thought about all of this for a while, trying to understand.

"It must have been summer to hide inside the stove," I finally said, with eight-year-old wisdom.

"You're right, Celia. You know, I never thought about that."

Mother didn't offer any more information, and although I was still puzzled, for now I had no more questions.

My father was six feet tall. He had bright blue eyes, dark hair, and a short, square mustache that always tickled when he kissed me. He was charming and dynamic, smiling and laughing easily and often. He was intelligent, generous, and loving. Other fathers were not like him, I thought.

Many people admired him. He was respected in the community, and people came to him for advice and sometimes for money. His intelligence, strength, and compassion attracted many acquaintances and friends, and he had the unique ability to accept all these people on their own terms. But the backbone of his philosophy of life was to be a law-abiding citizen and to be honest and straightforward at all times. I was absolutely convinced that he could conquer any obstacle and solve any problem. Certainly, he always found the exact words that would set my small world right.

Father was a successful businessman, yet he was modest

and unassuming. He saw to it that our home was comfortable and always cheerful. Our apartment at Hohe Weide 25 was large and sunny and furnished with tables and chairs of mahogany. Our maid Lena polished the furniture to a satiny gloss. As a very young child, I would take my dolls and play on the crossbars underneath the large dining room table, safely hidden by the fringes of the long, flowered tablecloth.

Father's work as an import-export merchant in wines provided us with summer vacations in Poland, Denmark, and other faraway places. While we did not live in luxury, our icebox was always stocked with food, and our closets were filled with clothing. All the extras, like music lessons, tennis, skating, and horseback riding, were taken for granted. It never even occurred to me to think that these expenses might be too much or to question whether they would deprive the family of other, more necessary items.

Father and Mother were deeply in love. I noticed the glances between them and Mother's quiet smiles—an understanding without words. Father's kisses for her seemed very different from the ones he placed on my cheek or forehead. They also had their private jokes and conversations, spoken in Polish so that Karin and I would not understand. Of course, we always resented this intrusion of a foreign language.

Mother was quiet and less outgoing than Father, but she was warm and affectionate. She was slightly over five feet tall, a little plump, with white skin, dark brown eyes, and silky black hair. She spent her days at home preparing meals for the family or out shopping for fresh food. Occasionally she would go downtown to Robinson or Tietz, the big department stores, and bring back beautiful wool and silk fabrics for coats and dresses for herself and for us. She knew exactly how she wanted us to look: a belt here, large buttons there, sometimes a white collar and cuffs. A seamstress would follow Mother's detailed instructions. While I grumbled and would have preferred more grown-up styles, Father always approved of her taste and selection. And it was his approval that was important to me.

During the weeks following our return from Bad Schwartau, I forgot about antisemitism and the pogroms. I was busy going to school, studying, and playing with friends. But by the middle of the school term in 1934, I had reason to remember Mr. Becker and Mother's story about hatred for the Jews.

By then, children we had known and had played with for years were suddenly calling us "Dreckjude." We heard this word everywhere—in parks, in stores, and on the streets. Even German children we didn't know purposely made remarks that we could hear: "Dirty Jews, Jude verrecke, Communist Jews." Non-Jewish neighbors appeared in brown SA (Sturmabteilung) or black SS (Schutzstaffel) uniforms and strutted about in their black boots, drinking a great deal, shouting at Jews, and yelling, "Heil Hitler." They no longer said good morning or good night to us. Was this what Mr. Becker had meant about Hitler's "taking care of the Jews"?

The flags on our street had also changed. Instead of the national flag or the occasional red flag bearing the hammer and sickle, all the flags were red with an emblem in the center called the Hakenkreuz (swastika). When I asked why the flags had been changed, I was told that these were now the only kind permitted by the authorities and that disobedience would be punished.

The hatred in the streets could be felt, and I developed a vague yet constant feeling of anxiety. The mood around us was somber. Nevertheless, there were almost whole days when life seemed bright and happy, when I would forget about the name-calling—only to be plunged once more into fear and darkness as passing Germans on the street shouted "Jude" and laughed at me. Each day, the walk to school grew longer and more worrisome.

Even at school I found no refuge from the daily reminders of our precarious existence. Our teachers constantly admonished us to be quiet on the streetcars, to avoid conversations with the neighborhood children, to stay out of fights, and to avoid drawing attention to ourselves in any way. Their repeated warnings left us with the impression that we were to be invisible. Because we were children? Or because we were Jewish? This was not clear, and our questions were never answered. We finally accepted the new set of rules, but I could not stop asking questions. Why were our neighbors calling us names? Why did they spit at us? Why did they hate us? Why did I have to walk so far to the Jewish school at Carolinenstrasse 35 when there was a school close to the house?

"All this is a passing phase," Father would say, "like the pogroms in Russia. And your school—it's a much better school; you'll be happier there."

I listened but was not convinced.

By the following year, 1935, my grades had begun to slip. I could not manage better than B's and C's. I couldn't concentrate; I was worried not just about the Germans but about what anybody might say or think about me. There were whispered conversations at home, some of them in Polish, none of which I understood. I asked if I could learn Polish, but Father always replied that French and English were enough. I cried often, seemingly without cause, dissolving into tears at the slightest remark. I knew that my parents were unhappy about the grades I received. In an effort to help me improve, they hired tutors, and this helped a little. The problem, however, was not with my ability but with my general frame of mind; I was assailed by constant fears and confusions.

That same year, my sister Karin started school.

I was four when Mother became pregnant. I wanted a little sister. Our old maid, Lena, promised me that if I left a cube of sugar on the windowsill for the stork every evening, he would bring me the sister I'd always wanted. And so he did! She was tiny and hardly ever cried. For the first two years, she used a language all her own, but she made sure that we understood what she wanted. Soon after her first birthday, she began to walk. But she didn't just walk; she seemed to strut instead, in her plaid dress with white collar and cuffs, gray stockings, and white-laced, high-top shoes. She laughed constantly and charmed everyone who came to know her.

For the first few weeks, she slept in my parents' bedroom, but it wasn't long before we began to share my large, sunny room. The walls were papered with a pink, flowery design, and the hardwood floor was polished and bare, except for two soft, white rugs near each of our beds. The windows were covered with starched, frilly white curtains. Mother and Father bought a large white bed for Karin that matched mine, along with a down quilt covered in pink satin. Our clothes were neatly stacked in a large white wardrobe with a full-length mirror. The rest of the room was filled with doll carriages, toys, and teddy bears.

Sharing my room with Karin was fun. I noticed that she watched my every move. By the time she was three, I had begun to tease her, pull her curly, blond hair, and laugh when she ran screaming to Mother. We played "Mommy," pushing our dolls around the house in a cream-colored doll carriage large enough for a real baby. We drew pictures on white sheets of paper with large crayons, and often we'd sing nursery rhymes with Mother. When Karin started school, we learned that she was an outstanding student with much promise. She was loved by her teachers and always surrounded by her many laughing friends.

After 1936, we traveled more frequently to Denmark than to the German resorts of Dunen or Wyk auf Föhr, where we had gone in the past. Even to a child, the contrast between Denmark and Germany was striking. The Danes were friendly. They laughed and had wonderfully rich food and ice cream. The return to Germany with its dark, somber atmosphere was always a shock, but eventually we would adjust again—or thought we had.

We also made frequent visits to Poland to see Mother's family, and I became especially fond of Grandmother, a small, white-haired woman. Although I could not understand her kind Yiddish words, I related to her warmth and love. She owned a busy grocery store, and I loved watching her talk to customers. I followed her around like a small puppy. If I stopped in front of the large jar with the red candy, Grandmother would eventually notice and give me one or two pieces, putting her fingers to her lips to let me know that this was our secret. She knew that Mother frowned on the eating of sweets between meals. Behind the store, Grandmother had a large, wonderful garden. Vegetables grew in long, straight rows. Adjacent to the garden were huge fields of red poppies. I would pick one, empty the ripe seeds into my palm, and eat them.

I often overheard Grandmother talking to my parents. I could not understand everything, but I gathered that she envied the fact that we lived in Germany, a country with good schools and a comfortable living, not to be compared with the poverty of Polish Jewry.

"But what about antisemitism?" Father interrupted one of these conversations. There was that word again. I listened carefully to Grandmother's reply, hoping finally to understand.

"We have lived with that for years," she began. "We don't know any differently. You will get used to it, too, and find that it is bearable after all." Grandmother sounded sure and convincing, but I still had questions.

"Why is hatred toward Jews accepted in Poland? Why, in Germany, do we have to get used to it?" I asked, using Grandmother's words. But I was dismissed with "This is not a topic for children."

It was not a topic I could dismiss, however, for antisemitism kept encroaching on our lives.

At home in Hamburg, Father's study was filled with books in all the colors of the rainbow, books that were beyond my comprehension, written in languages I did not understand.

The study was sacrosanct; there, Father's frequent evening visitors discussed and attempted to solve local and world issues. Most of the visitors, although friendly, were nameless faces to me—except for Rabbi Paul Holzer, who took the time to talk to me, and Martin Buber, who always picked me up and hugged me. I was allowed to say hello but not permitted to enter the study. Instead, I'd stand outside, look in through the half-closed door, watch the room fill with cigarette smoke, and listen to our visitors' subdued and serious discussion. Over and over again, they would talk about Germany, Hitler, antisemitism, Zionism, Palestine. . . . Now I knew about antisemitism not only through talk but experience, and I could easily connect the discussions in the study with the ever-increasing restrictions imposed upon the Jewish community.

In the fall of 1937, the administrators of our condominium at Hohe Weide 25 decided that Jews were no longer acceptable neighbors, and we, along with all of the other Jewish families in the building, were forced to leave our homes. We moved into a building owned by a Jewish man, Mr. Heilbut, on Hoheluftchaussee. Although we had almost the same amount of space, the neighborhood, more a commercial than a residential area, was not what we were accustomed to. We were surrounded by stores, shoppers, and noisy traffic. For me, the forced move was just one more proof of the power of the hatred for the Jews. Even my family seemed unable to fight the effects of it. Why did the Germans hate us so? What had we done? My mood grew darker.

After 1937, our school had to comply with many new rules and regulations. Many Jewish children from surrounding small towns were being transferred daily to our school.

It was in a poor neighborhood, with run-down houses and flats mainly occupied by working-class people. They were an unfriendly lot. Those whose windows faced onto our school-yard would yell to us at lunchtime, calling us obscene names —all ending in "Jude."

German authorities demanded lists of all pupils, including the names, addresses, and nationalities of their parents. Each of us was called by name, and we stood up to give our teachers the required information. Giving our addresses suddenly drew attention to the ethnic and economic differences among the various neighborhoods in the city. Even we children knew of these differences, either by instinct or because we had been told at home.

The question of nationality, however, was difficult to comprehend. I had never thought about it before. I knew that my parents had lived in Germany since 1921. I was told at home that we were Polish and retained current, valid passports. So, when my name was called, I carefully gave the required information: "Cecilia Landau, Hoheluftchaussee 25, nationality Polish."

Suddenly my classmates began laughing. What was so funny? Why was "Polish" funny? It made no sense. The next day I was told by several teachers as well as classmates that Polish Jews were dirty and uneducated, different from German Jews. But did it really matter where one was born or where one lived? Did it matter whether one was poor or rich? Being considered an outsider by my classmates was painful and demeaning to me. Some girls told me that now their parents were not sure that I was a proper playmate for them. I was crushed. Overwhelmed by pain, hurt, and confusion, I could not understand what I had done. First the non-Jewish neighbors, then strangers on the streets, and now my classmates hated me. I was constantly in tears, on guard, and alone.

One evening after Karin had gone to sleep, my parents called me into Father's study. I knew something special must be up.

"Celia," Father began, "have you heard about the children's transports to England?"

"Yes, I heard about them in school," I replied.

"There is a good chance that we can sign you up and that you could go to England," Father stated matter-of-factly.

I was stunned. Did they want me to go away?

"But why?" I asked.

"Well, there are lots of other children going to England, too. Life will be easier for you there."

It all seemed so vague—except the thought of leaving my parents. I went into a panic.

"Never, never will I go alone."

"Even though hundreds of other children are going?" Father asked.

"I don't care about other children...I will never go alone." I barely managed to get the words out. Mother put her arm around my shoulders.

"Won't you at least think about it?" Father persisted.

"No, never!" I screamed. "Never! Why do you want me to go?" I rushed out of the room and fell on top of my bed crying.

Mother followed, comforted me, and finally said, "Please, please don't cry. We will not force you. We just thought it would be a good idea." She kissed me and left. She did not tell me the reasons for its being a good idea, and I had no clear picture of what would have awaited me in England. It was only clear that I would be separated from my family and would be completely alone. I was petrified.

Hours later, still tossing and turning and thinking about the transport, I began to wonder if this meant that there was no hope for Jews in Germany. Yet my parents appeared to be living a contradiction. In spite of the realities that surrounded us, in spite of the foreboding inspired by the continued hate and fear that restricted and encompassed our lives, they remained hopeful. "Surely things cannot continue this way," they'd say. "All will take a turn for the better." It seemed impossible for my parents to believe that the hatred would be unrelenting or to understand the possible repercussions of it. But for one moment, lying on my bed, I knew that there was only one way out: to leave Germany—but not alone.

By 1938, my memories of the years prior to 1933 had faded. I no longer remembered a life without fear, without hateful glances on the streets, without being called "Jude." I no longer remembered sunny, carefree days of childish laughter, of pranks and fun. It seemed that life had always been foreboding.

Still, we had moments at home when we were able to deceive ourselves and pretend that no hatred or danger waited outside—moments when we managed to ignore our parents' worried faces and to believe that tomorrow morning all would be well. After all, I told myself, Father was there; he would always protect me. Even during Mother's brief hospital stay that summer, I clung to the illusion that Father would make sure that everything would turn out right.

Meanwhile, the world outside was becoming more and more dangerous. My own classmate, Ruth Moses, who lived on the other side of town, had been beaten savagely by six Hitlerjugend on her way home from school. These boys and girls were my age, wore white shirts and brown pants or skirts, and had been trained to hate, denigrate, and dehumanize Jews. They followed their leaders blindly and were encouraged to beat us without cause, to spit at us, to call us vile names. There was nothing we could do; we had nowhere to turn for protection or safety. We were at the mercy of their whims. Would I, too, be beaten because I was Jewish . . . or because I went to a Jewish school?

I prayed that we would leave for Palestine like the Baers or the Poppers. I could not sleep at night. Fear held me in its grip, but I did not know exactly what to fear. The dark? The people? The shouting? The neighbor children, their parents? I thought back to Bad Schwartau and the round table under the willow tree, the warm sun, the pink tablecloth, the strawberry tarts, and Mr. Becker's good-bye: "Hitler will take care of the Jews." Antisemitism, only a word five years before, had become the powerful force controlling our lives. Was it true, as Father had said, that only stupid people were antisemitic? But if these people were stupid, then why should any of it matter? I was terrified, but not only of the Germans around me. There was something else, something still unspoken and undefined, something yet to come. . . .

Benno ∾

1938–1941

The shrill ring of the doorbell woke us abruptly at 5:00 A.M. Karin and I got out of our beds. Barefoot, covered only by our long, pink nightgowns, we stood in our darkened room shivering, while Father opened the door. Mother stood right behind him, clutching her blue robe close to her body.

"Mr. Landau?" a voice asked.

Karin and I peered into the lit hallway and saw two policemen. Their green uniforms frightened us, and we stood close to each other, trembling. We could not follow their conversation, but from the bits and pieces we heard, we knew that we had to go to the police station—something about expired passports and our being Jewish Polish nationals.

I saw Mother whispering to Father. Her face was ashen. We moved a little closer and could hear Father explain to the two police officers that Mother had just returned from the hospital where she had had surgery. After further discussion, the policemen agreed to allow Mother to stay home with us, but they insisted that Father go with them.

It was October 27, 1938, and nothing in our little world would ever be the same. Father was going away. Now even our home would no longer be safe. Nothing seemed to make sense. I watched Father dress, kiss Mother, and come toward our room. He embraced us silently, then turned quickly and left with the two officers. Mother took Karin and me into our parents' large bed. Too frightened to speak, we cried quietly, holding each other and shivering, wondering what it all meant and what was going to happen.

By that afternoon, we had heard from friends that many Jewish Polish nationals had been detained downtown and would be deported to Poland. Our friends had no information beyond that; neither reasons nor time limits were given. During one of these phone calls, a friend advised Mother to pack some clothing for Father but not to bring the suitcase herself as she, too, might be detained.

I heard her ask, "Well, how else can I get the suitcase to Benno?" I knew the next part of the conversation concerned me because I heard Mother say, "But she's just thirteen."

She hung up and looked at me; she seemed worried and confused. I didn't wait for her to ask. "I want to go. Please let me. I promise to get the suitcase to Father and to return home as soon as I can."

I could feel her reluctance, her doubts, her indecision. All the fears I usually had when out alone on the streets were dissipated by my overwhelming desire to help Father—and to see him again. "Please, please," I pleaded, "you can trust me, I can do it, let me go . . ." I followed her down the hall as she found the suitcase and wearily began to pack it. "I can do it, Mother," I repeated, "I know I can." Tears rolled down her cheeks. Finally she sighed and nodded her head.

Supposedly more than a thousand men, women, and children were being detained in the courtyards of two Sammelplätze (collection sites) until the Germans could get them on trains to Poland. Mother wrote the addresses down and said, "Be careful, take the train downtown, and avoid talking to people on the way."

I dragged, pulled, and pushed the suitcase on and off the subway and then down the street until I finally reached the open gate of the first Sammelplatz. The courtyard was filled with men, women, and children, talking, gesturing, speculating. I looked for Father, asking anyone who was willing to listen to me, "Do you know where I can find Benno Landau?" They just shook their heads. I stood next to the now scuffed and dusty suitcase, feeling tired, forlorn, and baffled. What should I do? Suddenly I felt a hand on my shoulder and turned.

There was Father, still smiling, still tall, still strong. He hugged me and said, "I love you, Celia. What a courageous girl you are to bring such a heavy suitcase." I was choking back my tears. Almost immediately he began to push me away. "Please leave at once!" He was tense and insistent. "I do not want you here."

"But if I can leave, then why can't you come with me?" I asked. "Look, the gate is open. Many people are leaving. Why can't you come with me, Father?"

"It would not be the proper thing to do," he answered. He seemed to think about his answer for a second or two, perhaps recognizing the irony in his sense of decorum. Then he continued, "Please hurry and leave, and don't forget to take care of Mother!"

I walked to the gate and turned around for a last look. Father waved briefly and then disappeared into the crowd. I rushed home, knowing that Mother was waiting and worrying. I was also anxious to escape the hatred, name-calling, and spitting of the Germans on the street. I was sadder than I had ever been, yet proud that I had managed to deliver the suitcase.

About four days later, we had a letter from Father. He told us that the entire group of fifteen thousand Jews, from Hamburg as well as from other cities, had been taken by train and then pushed and shoved across the Polish border. He was in Zbaszyn, Poland, near the German border, staying with a local Jewish family, trying to obtain permission from the German authorities to return home. Weeks passed before we received another letter. Now Father said he saw no sense in staying near Zbaszyn and had decided to take the train to Sambor to stay with Mother's family. He wrote frequently, each time promising that he would get a reentry permit and return. He begged us not to be impatient. In the meantime, he asked us to pack the entire household and send all of it to his brother Herschel in Palestine. Surely, Father would be able to obtain certificates from the British government for all of us to go there.

Packing the entire household, however, was not a simple matter. We followed Father's wishes and hired a forwarding company, but the German government had rules against sending any new merchandise, gold, or money out of the country. So it was under the watchful eyes of two Nazi customs inspectors that we packed our belongings: furniture, china, linens, and personal clothing, even my maroon bike. Finally, two large wooden containers were sealed and taken to the harbor for shipment to Palestine.

Meanwhile, we waited for the certificate from Palestine and for Father to return. But the certificate did not come, and Father did not return.

One morning, two weeks after Father's departure, Karin and I set out for school on what at first seemed like just another day. Gradually, it dawned on us that the streets were quiet—too quiet. Something was terribly wrong. Near Rentzelstrasse, we met two of our classmates. They were in tears, and it took some time to find out why. They told us that during the night the Germans had vandalized all Jewish stores and had burned and desecrated synagogues, not only in Hamburg but throughout Germany. It was November 10, 1938.

For a long time, we stood there talking. Finally, we decided that school would undoubtedly be closed for the day, and we began to walk toward Bornplatz. We could smell smoke from the distance, and we saw large groups of police and SA near the synagogue. We didn't dare go any farther. We passed some small stores and saw shattered glass and merchandise strewn about the streets. Everywhere there were laughing Germans. Trying not to call attention to ourselves, we parted, each of us taking a different route home.

When we arrived, Mother already knew. A friend had called to tell her of the terrible destruction that had taken place and why it had happened. It had started in France with the desperate actions of a seventeen-year-old Jewish boy named Hershl Grynszpan. Like my father, his parents had been pushed over the German-Polish border on October 29, 1938. Separated from them, he was distraught and scared. In retaliation, he had shot a German official, Ernst vom Rath, in Paris. Now the Germans were bent on revenge.

Throughout Germany, the Gestapo (Geheime Staatspol-izei) began picking up Jewish men and carting them off to prisons, which turned out to be concentration camps near Berlin. There, these men were starved and beaten, and when they returned home six or eight weeks later, they were changed, fearful, sullen individuals desperate to get themselves and their families out of Germany. Some succeeded. But the devastation that came to be known as Kristallnacht left an indelible mark on all Jewish children. It was a horror never to be forgotten. Although school resumed a few days later, the mood was disruptive and disturbing. Almost daily, classmates or teachers announced that they were leaving for Palestine, South America, or the United States.

Mother wrote to Adolf, her older brother in San Francisco, who had left Poland when Mother was only three. She asked him to send us an affidavit so that we could come to the United States. She waited, fully expecting that Uncle Adolf would sponsor us and send the required documents so that we could find a safe haven in America. His reply was a short note of refusal. He explained that he could not possibly take on the responsibility of four people. Mother was angry and disappointed. This was not what she had hoped for or expected from a brother.

It was now eight months since Father had been sent to Poland. We lived a tentative day-to-day existence, always waiting for papers, always praying that he would return. Finally, in May 1939, we received a midnight telephone call: "I'm coming home. I have a permit for reentry. Meet me at the main train station."

He could not say exactly when he would arrive, so for the

next three days we met every train coming from Poland. The tall man with the gray hat—no, it was not Father. The tall man with the black suitcase—again a disappointment. On the third day, just as we were ready to give up, Father stepped off the train. He seemed taller and thinner than I remembered, but he was still smiling. As he embraced the three of us together, we all spoke at the same time, hugging, kissing, laughing, and crying. His presence made us forget everything else.

Then suddenly, he became serious and stern. "We have to obtain documents to get out of Germany, to get entry visas for Palestine or the United States. It has become urgent. There is no time to lose."

"When are we leaving?" I asked anxiously.

"Soon, very soon," Father replied.

However, it was more complicated than Father expected. Despite the fact that he continuously wrote, telephoned, and appealed to friends and relatives, neither the affidavit from the United States nor the promised certificate for Palestine arrived in the mail. The replies never varied: "Be patient. Don't worry. The documents are being sent." Still, weeks passed and nothing came.

Father's reentry permit into Germany, good for one month only, was about to expire. He managed to get it renewed by the German authorities with the promise that we would be leaving very soon. He had the permit renewed again in July. And a third time—or as the Germans pointed out, a last time—in August.

During the summer, we received notice from the local authorities that we had twenty-four hours to vacate our home. This time we had to move to furnished rooms in what had been designated as "Jewish buildings." We took our few belongings and, like gypsies, moved from one room to the next: Werderstrasse 5, Werderstrasse 7, Brahmsallee 15. These rooms were small and cramped, sparsely furnished with old run-down beds, a dresser, and a table. We shared kitchen and toilet privileges with as many as ten or twelve other occupants. Yet we had to be thankful to find even these places. We accepted the moving as a matter of course, without thinking about it, questioning it, or worrying. It was only temporary! Emigration papers were on the way, and we would be leaving very soon.

Indian summer that year was particularly hot, but Jews could no longer visit the beaches. Instead, we sat at home and waited for the mailman. Still nothing came. Then on September 1, 1939, strident sounds from loudspeakers all over the city proudly announced, "Germany has occupied Poland. We are at war and will soon be victorious." This was followed by the German national anthem, "Deutschland, Deutschland über alles."

Only one hour after the radio announcement, the doorbell rang and two men pushed their way into our apartment. In spite of the heat, they wore boots, hats, and long, black leather coats.

"Benjamin Landau? Gestapo."

This was our first face-to-face encounter with the Gestapo. From their reputation, we knew them to be ruthless, vicious, and brutal. They were capable of anything at any time and were accountable to no one but themselves. They bore no resemblance either in dress or manner to the local police who had come in October to arrest Father. They spoke in short, clipped, commanding tones that left no room for discussion. "You are an enemy alien and will be interned. Come with us."

The two men paced the floor while Father looked for his passport. He walked over to Mother to kiss her, but the Germans pulled him away.

"There is no time for that. Come, we have to leave."

Karin and I started to cry. Father looked at us with tears in his eyes. For the first time, even he seemed intimidated. Grabbing him roughly by the arms, the Gestapo dragged him out the door. Father was gone. Now Karin and I stood motionless and silent, lost in fear. Mother was sobbing uncontrollably.

Father was interned at Fuhlsbüttel, about ten kilometers from Hamburg. Only once, in 1940, and only to stop Mother's constant pleading letters and repeated trips to the Gestapo office did one of the officials permit us to see him at the Stadthaus in downtown Hamburg. Father looked thin and gray in his striped prison uniform. We just looked at each other silently, trying to smile. Only two feet separated us, yet we were not allowed to touch. Mother promised over and over that she'd keep trying to obtain emigration papers for all of us to leave Germany. "Don't give up," she said, "I'll find a way."

After that visit, letters from Father arrived less and less frequently. Sometimes more than four months would elapse before we'd get word. The message was always the same: "I'm well. I love you very much. Benno." However, each time he wrote, the postmark was different. It went from Fuhlsbüttel to Oranienburg, then finally to Dachau.

The winter of 1940 arrived with a vengeance, covering

Hamburg's canals with ice. Even the sun deceived us, pro-
viding little warmth. We no longer had heat and spent the
evenings wrapped in blankets and listening to the air-raid
sirens on those nights when the city was bombed. Food was
now rationed and in very short supply, especially for Jews.
Our ration cards were marked with a large "J" to identify us
as Jews. We had to shop in special stores, which were always
overcrowded, understaffed, and had limited supplies of food-
stuffs. Once a week, we stood in line and waited for hours to
receive the meager ration that still left us hungry.

We were also terribly short of money. The money in our
bank accounts had been confiscated, and our monthly allot-
ment was not enough to feed and clothe three people. Although I was still attending school during the day, I found a
job with a local store sewing dresses every night and on
weekends, even on the Shabbat. It no longer mattered. We
desperately needed the few marks I brought home to supple-
ment our income. Unfortunately, the job did not last; my
work was not proficient, and in a few short weeks, I was dismissed.

Life was a nightmare. The more successful the German
military advances were, the more aggressive were their hos-
tilities against us. I was not quite sixteen and was not only
terrified of the German SS and the Gestapo but of the Hitlerjugend bullies as well.

By the fall of 1940, Jewish children who had once been
smiling, boisterous, and happy had become quiet, serious,
and withdrawn. We lived constantly with fear, always looking over our shoulders. We were not allowed on the streets
after dark; being caught meant a beating, prison, or worse.
Parks, beaches, theaters, and movie houses were off limits to

Jews. We left the relative safety of our rooms only when it was absolutely necessary to go out.

One afternoon early in January, Mother and I sat, as we had on so many other days before, in the waiting room of the Jewish Community House on Beneckestrasse, hoping to be told that the necessary sum of $400 had been allocated through the Jewish Community Fund to get my father released from Dachau and to secure our passage out of the country. The room was filled with downcast and worried people, their anxious whispers repeating the same words over and over: entry visas... release... Shanghai... certificate for Palestine... Argentina... Brazil... even Honduras. Everyone was trying to get away.

The woman seated next to us, a stranger, turned excitedly to mother and asked, "Did you hear that a Jakob Leinfeld has been released? He was actually sent home from a concentration camp on the condition that he leave tomorrow for Italy! Actually released from a concentration camp!" she repeated, shaking her head.

At the sound of the man's name, Mother jumped up, grabbed my hand, and whispered, "Hurry, we must go home."

I looked questioningly at her, but her face was set in determined lines and I dared not ask why. As soon as we arrived home, Mother went to the telephone.

"Hello, Jakob? This is Sala. Is it true that you are leaving? Can I see you? Please. You have to tell me about Benno," Mother pleaded. "Just for a few moments?" she continued, almost begging, her voice filled with tears. "You saw him yesterday and I have not heard from him in weeks. This evening? Yes, we'll be there."

Mother turned to me. "Celia, it's true, Jakob Leinfeld was released from prison. Until yesterday, he and your father were sleeping on the same cot. You remember him, I'm sure. He and Father met years ago at various social functions, and he was sometimes a guest at our house. But only now, in prison, have they become close friends. He is leaving for Italy tomorrow, but he will see us tonight. He promised."

I knew that Mother would not ask Jakob how he had obtained his release. There seemed to be an unstated agreement that this information was not to be shared—no questions asked, no questions answered. Nevertheless, she appeared excited, and there was a hint of hope in her usually sad voice.

That evening we left our room to walk to Jakob's flat, a good thirty minutes away. Twilight was already throwing long shadows on the sidewalk. The air was cold and crisp, and we walked hurriedly and in silence. I was filled with anxiety, and I shivered as I thought of the old woman who had been found only a few days before, severely beaten and left to die. Attached to her coat was a scribbled, dirty slip of paper that read, "Out at night—dead by light."

I put this thought out of my mind, trying, instead, to recall Father's friend Jakob. I remembered a tall, heavyset, handsome man with blond, curly hair and clear blue eyes. He was about ten years younger than Father, always joking and laughing, enjoying life. He used to enter our house with the words, "I'm here, let's have a party!" Before the onset of the war, he had been wealthy and successful, the owner of one of the largest fruit import houses in Hamburg. But the Germans had confiscated his business.

It was almost dark when we arrived at the apartment

house on Isestrasse, took the elevator to the third floor, looked for his nameplate, and rang the bell. I hoped that we wouldn't stay long. The door was opened by a gaunt man with sunken, listless eyes and grayish-yellow skin. His shaven head glistened under the glare of the lamp. He smiled sadly through lips that bore the scars of many beatings. His upper front teeth were missing. He reached out, took Mother's hands in his, and held them tightly.

"Jakob?" Mother said uncertainly.

"Who else? Well, come in. But you can't stay long. Benno is fine, working. When I get to Italy, I will try to get entry papers for him." The words rushed out of his mouth. He sounded hurried and breathless, as if he had rehearsed these lines. He didn't ask us to sit down, and Mother seemed disappointed. But I was glad. I was worried about the curfew and felt restless and anxious to leave.

"But, Jakob," Mother asked, "have you looked in the mirror?"

"Don't worry," Jakob interrupted, "I'm all right. I'm fine, and I'll get the entry papers." But it was incomprehensible that this man would be able to help himself, let alone anyone else.

"Tell me more about Benno . . . ," Mother began.

"I have nothing else to tell you. I know nothing more, and even if I did, it wouldn't help you."

"What do you mean, it wouldn't help? When will I see Benno? Please tell us more. I'm sick with worry!"

"I don't know. I'm tired now, very tired. It would be best for you to leave . . ."

"Just like that, Jakob? Nothing more?" Mother's fluttering, outstretched hands were empty, suspended in midair.

Her shoulders slumped. She looked defeated, her eyes empty.

Jakob only shook his head. There were tears in his eyes. He embraced Mother and shook hands with me. We wished him a good journey and left.

It was completely dark outside. The moon and stars were hidden by clouds. The wartime blackout did not permit a single streetlight or uncovered window. The streets were deserted and silent. I was beside myself with fear. Mother and I held each other's hand tightly. Listening, hoping, and praying, we began groping our way home. Suddenly we heard the sound of clicking, running boots and a voice yelling, "HALT!" The Germans were already close behind us, pursuing their prey.

We started to run. In our haste and panic, Mother and I lost each other. For one frantic second, I knew that I was completely alone and running for my life. Flashlight beams twitched in search of their victims: Mother and me. I ran fast . . . faster . . . My foot missed the curb and gave way under a sharp pain in my ankle. I lay flat on my belly in the wet gutter, a messy stink covering the side of my face. Afraid to breathe, my eyes tightly shut, I wanted to scream. But a voice in my head kept repeating, "Don't move! Keep still!" I could hear them coming closer and closer. Then they were there beside me—running, still running. A stinging pain ran up my arm as boots fell heavily on my motionless hand. They passed me and rushed on.

Through half-opened eyes, I could see the still-searching beams growing dimmer and dimmer until they vanished in the night. Although the sound of their boots was no longer audible, I lay shaking in the filth, unable to move. In the distance, I heard Mother's frantic whispers calling my name.

My bruised fingers and broken ankle, set some days later, slowly healed, but the terrifying nightmares that began after that night kept recurring—night after night, week after week, month after month.

February 1, 1941, was my sixteenth birthday. It passed without a party, without a cake, without any mention. That night, in bed, I felt the pains and heard the growling of my empty stomach. Unhappy and lonely, I cried myself to sleep.

Three weeks later, on February 21, 1941, at about 5:00 P.M., I heard a sharp, impatient ring of the doorbell. Two men with cruel, unsmiling faces confronted me. I knew who they were even before they spoke the dreaded word *Gestapo* and pushed their way inside.

"Where is Mrs. Landau?"

I pointed toward the kitchen and followed them.

"Mrs. Landau?"

Mother nodded her head. The taller of the two carelessly dropped a small wooden cigar box on the table. The lid was held down with a rubber band. Mother and I stared at the box without comprehension.

"Ashes," the voice said impatiently, "Benjamin Landau's ashes from Dachau. He died on January 31."

Something was burning on the kitchen stove. The foul smell engulfed us as we stood motionless, our eyes fixed on the cigar box. Mother's face was white; she looked old and frail. She started to cry and moan. Karin, bewildered, rushed into the kitchen. Then Mother screamed, "They killed your father! God, where are you? How could you let this happen? Why have you abandoned us? And I believed in your mercy..."

Burial took place on February 23, 1941. The February winds blew icy gusts across our tearstained faces as we stared at the open grave, a gaping black hole in the stony, frozen ground. Rabbi Carlebach was giving the eulogy for Benno Landau: "a wonderful, generous man, whose life has been snuffed out at age forty-eight..." Was he really talking about my father? I saw only the unfinished pine coffin and pictured the small cigar box inside, fastened with a rubber band and filled with ashes. But whose? My father's? The rabbi's voice receded; I did not want to hear his words. I closed my eyes and saw the past and my father, the Benno Landau I knew and loved. Simultaneously, I heard the scraping sounds of metal against soil and then the crackling and thudding of the earth as it was strewn on top of the coffin. Now the rabbi's voice came to me loud and strong, as he began to recite the prayer for the dead. Through uncontrollable sobs, I repeated after him, "Yitgadal veyitkaadash shemei raba ..."

Sala ∽

1941–1942

Frosty windows sparkle
covered with
snow flowers
glistening in the night.
We cower in a dark corner
and our steamy breaths
fill the chilly room.
Even the bucket
of water
is covered with ice.
Our ears listen
to the Germans' steps
outside
marching back and forth
beneath our window.
Frosty windows sparkle
covered with
snow flowers
glistening in the night.

By the fall of 1941, Jewish adults and children alike had been ordered by the Germans to wear the yellow star on their coats. We were now even more easily identified as objects for beatings, ridicule, and harassment.

Then, on the afternoon of October 21, 1941, we received a registered, official envelope from the Gestapo offices in

Hamburg: "You are ordered to appear on October 25, 1941, at the Sammelplatz for resettlement. Take only one suitcase per person." Rumor had it that about twelve hundred of us would be evacuated and resettled in Litzmannstadt—or Lodz, as it was called in Polish. But no one seemed to know why.

In any case, we did not have the privilege of choice. We packed whatever we could and gave the rest away to friends and Jewish neighbors. Hardly anyone wanted our leftovers; they knew their turn would come. Our friends, the Fromms, walked us into the building of the Pronvinzialloge für Niedersachsen, Moorweidenstrasse, and kissed us good-bye. Hours later, we were herded out of the building into trucks and transported to the waiting trains. There, we were pushed into compartments with sealed windows. We heard the Germans lock the doors from the outside.

The compartments were crowded, stuffy, and hot, and tempers were short. Children whined, and grown-ups were impatient—except for Mother. Although Karin whimpered in her arms, she seemed calm, as though resettlement in Poland, even under these adverse conditions, was almost welcome. Poland was, after all, her place of birth, and her memories were of Poland in the prewar days. Perhaps this return to familiar surroundings would give her some measure of comfort. Ever since Father's death, Mother had been withdrawn and apathetic. But now, anticipating the change, she seemed to be more in the present.

Across from us sat an elderly couple. Quietly resigned, they held hands throughout the journey. They were short and heavyset. His bald head glistened with perspiration; her wavy, fading red hair was just beginning to turn gray. She smiled frequently and gave us several pieces of candy.

After a long and distressing journey, jolting noises brought us to attention. When the train finally came to a full stop, the doors were thrown open, and we peered outside into the bright midday sun.

"Raus, hurry, this is the end of your trip. Your suitcases will come later." The Germans kicked and beat us as we hurried past them out of the compartments. We waited outside the cars, facing a group of about thirty men in black uniforms and black caps with an orange band. Like us, they wore a yellow star on their coats.

"Jewish ghetto police," someone whispered.

We had arrived in Lodz, Poland. The police lined us up, and we began to walk. Although we straggled and complained, there were no wagons or cars for the elderly or the children. Next to Mother walked a young man in the ghetto police uniform. They began talking in Polish, and although I did not understand, I guessed that Mother was asking a lot of questions. She sounded relieved, seemingly not aware of the horror of our new situation. I, however, saw only the dilapidated houses, the huts, and the filth around us. The shabbily dressed men and women of the ghetto stared at us through dull, unsmiling eyes. The cobblestoned streets were in need of repair, the walkways were unpaved, and the open sewers were filled with vile-smelling raw sewage. Four men and two women passed us, pulling a heavy, long, metal drum as though they were horses. Clad in reeking rags, they left an unbearable stink in their wake. I learned later that they received double bread rations for cleaning the outhouses.

After about two hours, our straggling column came to a halt on Mlynarska Street. The building immediately in front of us was set back behind a courtyard and resembled a school. The ghetto police explained that we would be housed in classrooms until permanent rooms could be found. Our daily food ration would consist of a bowl of soup and a slice of bread. We were to sleep on the floor on blankets, using our coats for cover. There were no bathrooms, only outhouses downstairs in the backyard.

Next to us on the hard floor was the elderly couple we had met on the train. Their names were Julie and Julius. Mother made her bed between Karin and me and slept fitfully. During the long weeks that followed, there were many nights when I would cry out in the dark and Julie's arms would comfort me. Her warmth and love were heartfelt and were given spontaneously and unconditionally. She told me over and over about her son Dan, who had escaped from Germany in 1939 on the SS *Orinoco,* the last boat of immigrants to be allowed to enter Cuba. After his American quota number was called in 1941, he had continued on to New York. She said that she and her husband would meet him there, and together they would walk down Broadway. I nodded my head, believing that it really would happen.

Mother was constantly worrying that Karin and I did not have enough to eat. The food ration in Hamburg had been inadequate; now, the meager ration in the ghetto was even less than our ever-hungry stomachs were accustomed to. At first, Mother bartered some German marks for more bread and a little margarine, but our marks soon ran out. After that, she began sorting through our clothing, trying to find any item that we could spare to trade for food. It wasn't long before we were left with only the barest necessities.

After six weeks, we were assigned to various rooms throughout the ghetto, with five to eight people in a room.

Julie and Julius were quartered with five others on Zgierska Street, while we moved to Pawia Street. We shared a small room there with two elderly couples, the Perlmanns and the Heilbronns from Berlin.

The room was freezing, but there was no coal to feed the empty, black iron stove. We wore layer upon layer of clothing to keep warm, but this only provided a nesting area for colonies of typhus-carrying lice. Three wood-slatted cots, one to a family, were jammed into the room. My sister and I slept on either side of Mother. Karin, now eleven, was terrified of the long, dark nights. She whimpered constantly, scared to death of the bedbugs, which gathered during the day on our filthy ceiling, then dropped during the night, one by one, onto our bedding. They made tiny, plopping, cracking sounds, and their bloody marks on our pillows and blankets left a vile, sickening smell.

Our "toilet" was a bucket in the corner. We had no curtain to hide our crouching bodies; we urinated in degrading shame. In the mornings, the full bucket had to be carried downstairs to the yard and emptied. We had decided to take turns, but Mr. Perlmann saw to it that my sister and I made most of these trips. "After all, you are young and strong and ought to help your elders!" He knew we would not argue.

The winter evenings were sad and quiet, and we huddled together for comfort and warmth. The icy wind shivered outside and blew through the cracks around our small window. Our breathing sent whirls of steam into the chilly air. Even the large pot of fresh water from the pump downstairs had a thick crust of ice. On some nights, I would stand at the windowpane tracing the sparkling frost flowers and making up poems and stories, some full of wishes and dreams, some full of jarring, angry words.

The relentless sound of marching boots as the Germans passed back and forth on the pavement below reminded us that we were always being watched. Red-and-white-striped German guardhouses, spaced at regular intervals, stood just on the other side of the barbed-wire fence that separated the Jewish ghetto from the Polish neighborhood. Over there, the bakery still sold bread. Every morning I'd see Poles carrying home their warm loaves, while our bodies grew thinner and thinner. I would often imagine the aroma and the taste and wish for the miracle of just one slice. Within four months of our arrival in the ghetto, many of those who had come with us on our transport had already died of typhus, dysentery, and starvation.

Almost immediately after our arrival, Mother's renewed spark of interest in life disappeared. As her health began to fail, she became weak and listless. Her feet began to swell, and her face became puffy. Her mind often seemed to be wandering; she would look at us and smile, as if she had escaped to some happier place. During the long nights, I suffered from the harsh realization that she might not survive. In the mornings, I denied this fact, even to myself. By December, Mother's swollen, heavy body lay stretched out on the wooden cot all day. Her face was disfigured and her eyes sunken and dull. Her breath came in slow, wheezing spurts. Day after day she gaped at the ceiling as if in a trance. She no longer spoke. January 5, 1942, was her fiftieth birthday, but we did not celebrate it. Her face was flushed and burning, and she was not aware of us or of her surroundings.

She cared little about food. Only once did she consent to see a doctor.

"Hunger, starvation—I can't help," he had said and shrugged. "I'm sorry."

I watched her, remembering the good years. Was it possible that only five years had passed? Those happy times now seemed incredibly far away. Aloud I had always called her Mother, but to me she was Sala. Even as a small child, I had loved the sound of her name and had whispered it over and over. Sala had been a beautiful, dark-haired woman with sparkling brown eyes, an easy smile, and gentle words. She had lavished concern and attention on her husband and children. Her contagious sense of humor would send us both into fits of uncontrollable laughter. When I cried, her arms held me, and I would bury my face in the thick, dark perfumed hair that hung over her shoulders. I loved to hear her talk about her childhood in Poland. The youngest of seven children, she had come from a close, loving family, all of whom had spoiled little Sala.

These were my memories of how Mother had been, until the day in 1939 when the Gestapo arrested my father. Then, this quiet, gentle, passive person began to reveal a previously hidden strength, endurance, and determination. Week after week, all alone, she had fearlessly trekked to Gestapo headquarters and stubbornly pleaded with the Germans to obtain Father's release. She had only one goal: to get Father out of prison. Her efforts had come to an abrupt end when the two Gestapo officers had marched into our kitchen, nonchalantly dropped a wooden cigar box on our kitchen table, and carelessly remarked, "Ashes from Dachau—Landau!"

Now Sala lay almost lifeless on the cold, narrow cot.

One day my coworker, Lolek, gave me a gift: a coupon for a bag of potato peels to be redeemed at the local soup kitchen on Lutomierska Street. I was overjoyed, and that evening after work I went to collect them.

The lines outside the kitchen door had already formed; they stretched almost the entire length of the block. I waited anxiously and impatiently while the snow seeped into my shoes. I prayed that they would not run out of peels before it was my turn. I was lucky: three hours later, I received my precious treasure wrapped in old paper. Once outside, a wet, sticky fluid ran through the sopping bag and over my hands and coat. The strong, pungent smell reminded me of decaying garbage. I gagged. But my frozen fingers clung to my treasure, and I stubbornly trudged home, my feet icy and numb. Slowly I climbed the dark stairs and entered our small, dimly lit room. Silence greeted me. No one seemed to notice. I took a bucket and went downstairs to the pump. The iron pump handle was cold and stiff, difficult to move. Each bucket of water required a tremendous effort. Bucket after bucket of clean water washed over the peels. I pushed them down, discarded the dirty water, and pumped more clean water over them. When, after countless buckets, the peels still felt sandy and grimy, I was too exhausted to pump any longer.

Upstairs in the corner of our room stood an old meat grinder that had been there when we moved in. It had been years since there had been any meat to grind, but it worked fine for potato peels. With a little flour and salt, I was able to form patties. Our roommates sat quietly on their cots, their eyes riveted to the peels and filled with envy. But there was not enough to share. I felt guilty, until I remembered that they had not shared the loaf of bread that they had gotten in exchange for a bartered gold watch. This evening the single-burner stove gave off enough heat to warm the iron frying pan, the bottom of which was covered with last week's rancid ration of a brown, linseed-like oil. Slowly the patties fried to a dark brown color, while smoke curled toward the ceiling and made the steamy room smell sour and unpleasant. On our plates, however, the patties looked delicious. Karin even smiled as we chewed the gritty, tasteless, sticky mess.

Suddenly Mother sat up, fascinated by the brown patties, her eyes shiny and following my every move. I gave her a plate and fork, and she even tried to eat. We looked at each other, and for a brief moment, we were together in the sunny, large kitchen of our home in Hamburg. It was breakfast time and I was seven, skinny and tall, still growing, still refusing my breakfast of rolls with butter and jam that Sala had so carefully prepared. Angry and frustrated, she had sputtered, "One day, Cecilia, you'll be grateful for potato peels!" How I'd laughed—potato peels! Imagine, potato peels!

Just as suddenly as this vision had appeared, it was gone. Now tears ran down Mother's sunken cheeks. Gently, I touched her face with my fingers and wiped away her tears.

Filled with work, worry, and hunger, the days and weeks crawled by almost unnoticed. Spring surprised us one morning, as winding rivulets carried the melting snow down the crowded streets and sidewalks. It was April 1942. Unexpectedly, the Jewish ghetto administration posted deportation lists. Since we had been sent from Germany, were assumed to be German Jews, and were also among the most recent arrivals, we were scheduled for deportation along with Julie,

Julius, and many others from our transport. As much as we hated the ghetto, we were afraid to leave it. When Mother realized that we might be deported, she urged me to do whatever I could so that we might stay. I doggedly went from one Jewish ghetto official to another to prove our Polish nationality. Finally, we were granted permission to remain in the ghetto. We considered ourselves fortunate. At least here we knew what to expect; the unknown might be worse. But most of the German Jewry, including Julie and Julius, were not spared. In a frenzy, I rushed over the wooden bridge that divided the ghetto to see them before they left. We had become close friends, and our farewells were difficult. Julie and I embraced and kissed each other, and once again she reminded me to look for her son if I reached New York before she did. I nodded sadly and left. I was convinced that I would meet Julie and Julius again. But no word of the deportees ever reached the ghetto. And the postcard Julie promised never arrived.

One evening in May, Mother grabbed my hand and held it for a long time. "Cecilia, promise me, please, when I'm gone that you'll take care of Karin. There is no one else . . . it will be up to you . . ." Her voice trailed off. Her dark, heavy eyes glistened.

I looked at Sala and nodded.

"Promise," she repeated, "I want to hear your voice."

"I promise I will take care of Karin," I said in a whisper, meaning it with all my heart. Sala relaxed, dropped my hand, closed her eyes, and resumed her painful, heavy breathing. It was the last time she was aware of us.

I knew that not much time was left, yet I dared not think about it. But it was impossible to escape thoughts of death.

The reminders were constant: the skinny, ragged wagoner was seen day after day picking up the ghetto dead. He rode from street to street on his rickety little black wagon drawn by a tired, hungry horse.

On July 13, 1942, he stopped at our door. I was returning home from work, tired and listless, when I saw the black wagon. I rushed up the stairs, taking them two or three at a time, hoping, praying, but already knowing the worst. The driver stood in the middle of the room surrounded by our roommates and neighbors. Karin stood in the corner, alone. I looked at her sad face, then quickly turned to the cot. Mother was covered with a sheet. I could no longer see her face. No one spoke. The wagoner pushed me aside, wrapped the sheet around Mother, and carried her downstairs to the wagon. I stood riveted to the floor. I felt nothing, yet I wanted to scream.

"Poor orphans," the neighbors from across the hall whispered. I walked over to Karin and clutched her hand. Her blue eyes were moist, her mouth tightly closed, and her face ashen. I wanted to talk to her, but I couldn't find the words. Suddenly, the room was empty, and we were alone.

Karin and I waited for word from the cemetery about Mother's burial, but we heard nothing. A week later, on Sunday, we decided to make the two-hour walk to the cemetery at Marysin to find out what had happened. We walked in silence, lost in painful thoughts, feeling empty and helpless. Fear, hunger, and sadness had taken their toll.

We crossed over the wooden bridge to the other side of the ghetto. Below the bridge, the Polish streetcars ran back and forth, guarded by Germans with rifles. An open, horse-drawn droshky caught my eye. It carried a smiling family in their Sunday best. A small infant in a pink dress was resting on a large, lace pillow. They were on their way to church for a christening. We had only burials. . . .

Finally, we reached the cemetery. In front of the administration building, an old man sat on a broken chair. He looked at us and knew immediately why we had come.

"We have more dead bodies than spaces to bury them. Even the walkways have been used for graves. You have come for nothing. Go home, children! Today no one buries the dead."

We listened to the bent-over man, his long beard waving from side to side as he spoke, but nevertheless we walked on toward the building. As we entered the huge hall, the strong, sickening odor of decay and death filled our nostrils. Piles of bodies stretched as far as the eye could see, each body placed between two narrow wooden boards that were tied together with coarse string. A name tag was attached to each greenish, decomposing ankle. We searched among the dead bodies of men, women, and children until we managed to find the one that bore Mother's name: "Sala Landau." Her swollen, bare feet protruded from the boards.

Without a word, we moved toward the two shovels that leaned against the far wall; then we went outside to search for a small unused plot. We found a tiny area and began to dig in the dry, stony earth. We spent hours in the July sun, the silence broken only by the scratching of the shovels against the dirt. When the hole in the ground finally seemed large enough, Karin took my hand, and we walked back to the great hall. We pulled and pushed and shoved corpses until we were able to lift Mother's body, heavy and cold with death, out of the pile. We carried her outside to the freshly dug hole and lowered her into the open grave, barely big enough to embrace her body. For a few painful moments, we stared at the planks and at the exposed feet, not yet able to part with the dead. Then we carefully filled the grave with earth and sand until only a small mound was visible. Using a stick, we scratched her name and dates of birth and death onto an oblong wooden marker that we found nearby. We placed it into the dry soil. We stood motionless and drained, staring at the grave. We had no tears and no prayers for our dead mother.

Karin ~

1942

> *A place without children:*
> *No children laugh,*
> *No eyes twinkle,*
> *No girlish tears,*
> *No feet are skipping,*
> *No faces plead,*
> *No boys make mischief,*
> *No warm hands reach:*
> *There are no children.*
> *The Germans tore our hands*
> *From theirs,*
> *And they disappeared*
> *In the distance.*
> *Truck, after truck, after truck*
> *Of smiling,*
> *Crying,*
> *Children.*
> *Never to be seen again.*

*I*t was the fall of 1942; we had been living on Pawia Street in the Lodz ghetto for eleven months. Karin and I had watched Mother die of starvation. Only eighteen months earlier, we had buried a cigar box full of ashes—supposedly the remains of our father.

Karin seemed to recover from the death of our father, but Mother's death left her profoundly changed; now, she neither spoke nor smiled. When we buried Mother, it was as if we had buried a part of Karin as well. The Karin I had once known, the slim, blond, blue-eyed girl with a ready smile, bubbling words, and an exuberance for life and learning, was now unreachable, lost in a silent stupor. Whenever we left our room, she held my hand tightly, as if fearing yet another separation.

Now, with Mother and Father dead, I was Karin's sole support. Mother's last words haunted me day after day: "Promise me that you'll take care of Karin when I'm gone!"

I was determined to keep my promise. But it was more difficult than I could have imagined. Despite my seventeen years, I was still a child and hardly knew what it meant to take care of a twelve-year-old sister. There were rumors of small ghetto "schools" hidden away in factories. There, she could be with other children and receive an extra midday soup. More importantly, the "school" was a place where she could be registered as a worker. To the Germans, this was considered absolutely essential. Jews were worthy of life only if they were able to work. It was risky, however, since schools had been forbidden by the Germans. The chances of being caught were great and punishment severe.

Nevertheless, I decided to find out, and I tediously made the rounds of different production centers. It was more exacting and complicated than I had anticipated. Nothing was easy in the ghetto. The managers of most factories at first denied the existence of "schools." When they finally broke down and admitted that such a program was available, they invariably gave other excuses: "Our quota is filled.... We have no openings available.... Try another factory.... Maybe you will have more luck a year from now." One manager asked what I would give him in return if he found a place for my sister. When I explained that I had neither money nor valuables, he laughed and said that that was not what he had in mind. I was stunned. The realization was sudden and painful: there were favors to be bought, but they had to be paid for one way or another—even among our own.

Finally, after weeks of effort and with the help and intervention of our neighbors, Judge and Mrs. Neuman, who contacted numerous people of influence, I managed to find Karin a place in a factory. It was a small shop that produced ladies' hats for the Germans. They "employed" young children, keeping them in a separate room under the pretense of work but actually teaching them arithmetic and Hebrew. Every evening, however, Karin still returned to our room sad and depressed.

"Please tell me about your day at the factory," I would plead. "How many other children are there? Are the teachers nice? Do you get your soup at noontime? Do you speak German to the other children, or are you learning Polish?"

She would not speak; her misery remained locked up. What was she thinking? Her pain was understandable, but why didn't she speak? At night, after eating her meager rations, she'd go to bed and cry herself to sleep. Her muffled sobs only added to my own guilt and sadness.

Almost six weeks had passed since Mother's death, and I was still unable to take care of Karin. I, too, felt pain and loss. Mother's pleading eyes and her haunting last words followed me day and night, a constant reminder not only of my loss but also of the responsibility for which I felt inadequate.

Then, at the beginning of September, a new proclamation

was pasted on doors, walls, and posts throughout the ghetto. Large crowds of curious readers gathered and stood in silence, unable to comprehend fully the implications of the words: "Effective September 5, 1942, there will be a Gehsperre (curfew) in the ghetto. No one will be allowed to leave their respective buildings. Factories will be closed until further notice, and the Germans will run inspections from street to street and house to house."

We had always been restricted to the ghetto, and we had grown accustomed to the many laws that regulated our daily lives, but this total confinement to our building was new. The air was charged with fear. This latest bulletin overshadowed everything else: something terrible was about to descend upon us.

"What do you think it means?" I asked our neighbor Eta.

"Who knows, who can predict? But I know for sure that when they come, I will hide the baby," she whispered.

"Why? What do you think they'll do? Where will you hide little Rachel?"

Eta did not respond.

"And Karin? What should I do about Karin?"

"Don't worry, she's twelve years old. She'll be all right."

But I was not convinced. We sat in our rooms, tense and apprehensive. I thought that perhaps when the Germans came, Karin and I could run through the backyards into another street. But then what? Where to hide? How could one escape the Germans?

"Karin, what do you think?" I prodded. "What should we do?"

She merely shrugged her shoulders and maintained her silence. Her sad half-smile tore my heart. She had withdrawn into some other world, and I was unable to reach her. It had to be my decision alone. In an agony of panic and fear, I weighed the alternatives and realized that it would be useless to run. The Germans were all around us. We would stay; we would wait and hope.

So we sat in our stuffy room, while outside the sky was blue and the sun bright and warm. Eta's husband, Julek, spent the days on the roof of the building as our lookout. It was quiet until the third day after the poster had appeared, when the Germans came with their trucks and their dogs. Julek shouted, "They are on Pawia Street now! They will be in front of our building in another five or ten minutes!"

We waited. For some inexplicable reason and in spite of the warm day, we put on our coats. I knew that the Germans would allow those of us they considered good workhorses to survive. And I realized that Karin would have to look older than she actually was in order to pass for an able-bodied adult and thus be less at risk than a child.

"Today you, too, can wear lipstick and rouge!" I told her. For the first time in weeks, a smile crossed her face. Quickly I applied powder, rouge, and lipstick. She seemed to enjoy the attention and the change in her face. When I looked at her, I could hardly recognize my little sister.

The loudspeaker blared through the silent afternoon: "Everyone, raus, outside. Line up in the courtyard!"

We rushed downstairs, the young, the old, the children, all of us, anyone able to walk. There were about sixty of us from our building. We stood and waited while the Germans with their barking, panting dogs searched for those who might have disobeyed orders. Those who had hidden were quickly tracked down and immediately herded into the waiting trucks. The Smulewicz brothers, Bronka Berminc and her old father, and Motek Fischer were brought out, confused and trembling.

About six Germans watched us intently. The one immediately in front of us used his rifle as a pointer and began his selection, going hurriedly down the line of human beings waiting to be sentenced. "You to the right, you to the left, you to the right!"

It took only minutes. He pushed Karin out of line and signaled her to the left. I noticed that about half of our small group had been pushed to that side, most of them either very old or very young.

"Those on the left, into the truck!"

I could not see Karin in the crowd of those being pushed onto the trucks, but once she was on the truck, we caught sight of each other. Her eyes were widened with fright, and I could see her trembling. But she did not utter a sound. I stepped toward the truck, only to be pushed away with the barrel of a rifle. We were only inches apart, our hands grasping for each other, yet those inches might as well have been miles. The motors started up, and the trucks began to pull away.

I felt faint. Karin's eyes remained locked onto mine until I could no longer see her. My hysterical sobs and tears mixed with those of the others who had lost brothers, sisters, fathers, mothers, husbands, wives, and children.

Slowly, our small remnant dragged upstairs—except for Eta and Julek, who raced up the stairs three steps at a time. Before we reached the landing, loud shrieks pierced the air. We rushed into their room. The middle drawer of the old, high chest, which had obviously been made up and locked as a hiding place for little Rachel, was now pulled open. Julek stood like a statue, blank and frozen, beside his wife. Eta, still shrieking, held the baby in her arms, its tiny face a transparent blue from suffocation.

We tried to console them, to hold Eta and the baby, but Eta's cries of anguish did not stop. Finally, we left them to their grief.

The three Rabinowicz sisters, who lived in the room adjacent to ours, came to my door, their faces stained with tears, their sobs filling the room. They had lost both their parents. "Now you are completely alone," they said to me. "Come, move in with us."

I nodded agreement and took my few belongings while they moved my cot. I was thankful that they wanted me.

How many men, women, and children had been taken out of the ghetto? Where were they taken? And why? Everyone had lost at least one member of the family, and in some cases entire families had disappeared. I inquired at the ghetto police station about Karin but got no answers. No one seemed to know. Karin was gone. Should we have hidden after all? Was there something else I should have or could have done? Where was she now?

I spoke to an empty room, asking my mother to forgive me, asking Karin not to cry, promising her we would be together—somehow. It was impossible even to imagine that we would never see each other again.

Szaja ~

1942–1944

Night after night
You stood
Outside my door,
Silent and sad.
I did not know.
When finally
We met
Under blazing stars
I could not find
The words
To say
What I felt in my heart.

Weeks went by, and I still had no word about Karin. My job in the ghetto provided the only distraction from the ongoing nightmare of her absence. Ten months earlier, an engineer named Adolf Goetz had been able to convince Chaim Rumkowski, the head of the Jewish ghetto adminis-tration, that the ghetto needed beautification and improve-ment. Goetz had assembled a group of former architects and engineers to draw up plans for new housing, parks and trees, schools and playgrounds.

Before the war, Goetz had been our neighbor in Hamburg. In the ghetto, he had given me my first job in his new office at Rybna 8, where I worked as a clerk and was responsible only to him. Sometimes he would launch small paper airplanes from his desk to mine. Concealed inside were short, sometimes funny, sad, or sentimental poems. In spite of my many mistakes, he never scolded me. He was kind, intelligent, and lovable. I was very grateful.

There was merit to Goetz's beautification plan, but it was basically a crazy notion. He seemed to have forgotten that the Germans had imprisoned us in this place called the ghetto. Indeed, he was one of the few dreamers still among us—until this illusion of normalcy was brought to an abrupt halt.

For months, whispers and rumors had been flying around the office suggesting that Rumkowski had lost interest in our project and would close it down. We had speculated and worried. Finally, Engineer Goetz confronted us with the actual news.

"As of next week, on Monday, our office will cease to exist. Der Alte, Chaim Rumkowski, decided. And in spite of my pleading and cajoling, he stood firm. He leaves me no choice but to tell you that as of next Monday, there will be no jobs and no soup for any of us. Just like that..." His voice faded. The statement left us stunned.

As he made the announcement, tears ran down Goetz's wrinkled, leathery cheeks. His skin hung loosely over his high cheekbones. He was barely five feet tall, but on his shoulders rested an enormous, grotesque head. His wire-framed glasses could not hide his always red-rimmed, squinting eyes. He spoke fast and with a slight lisp. To me, at seventeen, he seemed ancient, but he was probably no more than about sixty-five years old. Once he had been a cheerful man; now he was old and broken, his dream shattered.

Before Adolf Goetz had given me my job, I had spent weeks going from one factory to another: the straw factory where they manufactured large shoes to be worn by the German soldiers in the Russian snows; the garment factory where uniforms were sewn; even the metal factory where utensils for the army were produced. The answers had never varied: "Sorry, we cannot employ you. Our directives come from the Department of Labor." I had made repeated trips to the Labor Department offices and had seen the director himself, Leonard Luft, but he had no work for me. After my third visit, he had rewarded my persistence by throwing me out of the office with a harsh "Raus! Don't you dare come back!"

Now I thought I might have to go through those degrading experiences once again. But as Adolf Goetz shook hands with me to say good-bye, he whispered, "We have about one more week before we close up shop. Wait a few days and then go downstairs to the second floor. They may have an opening, or perhaps they can help you find some sort of work."

Once again, I was grateful to him.

"But what will you do now?" I asked.

"The devil knows; at my age, it hardly matters."

A week later he was found dead in his room. He had died of hunger, they said, but most probably he had lost all desire to live. Only five coworkers made the long trip on foot to the cemetery at Marysin to attend his burial. I was among them. I stood at his graveside with tears in my eyes. I would miss Adolf Goetz.

It was Monday. Two weeks had elapsed since I lost my job, and here I was back in the office at Rybna 8, waiting and hoping that I would be lucky enough to land another job and a chance for midday soup. The day was unseasonably cold for November. Although the pot-bellied stove was barely warm, I still embraced the long iron stovepipe, trying to squeeze a last bit of heat from its black, shiny metal. But it yielded nothing; the day's coal ration had been used up.

Out of the corner of my eye, I saw a bespectacled man sitting behind a desk, staring at me. I wondered how long he had been watching me. His scrutiny seemed like an invasion of my privacy, and I wanted to run. But I stood my ground. He got up, walked toward me, stopped in front of the stove, and stretched out his hand.

"I am Szaja Spiegel."

"I'm pleased to meet you," I replied in formal Polish. "My name is Cecilia Landau."

He looked at me silently for several minutes.

"I heard that you need work. Maybe I can be of help. In about two weeks, I'll head a new office and need clerks and secretaries."

I could hardly believe my luck. Had Adolf Goetz arranged this, too?

"Really, you're not joking?"

"Honestly, I promise." He sounded convincing. I looked at him again, seeing him as if for the first time. He was in his late thirties, slim, of medium height, with straight, black hair and dark brown eyes. He wore thick, black-rimmed glasses. He looked serious; there was no smile on his lips. "Come to room 204 in two weeks. I'll be waiting for you."

"Thank you. I'll be there—I'm counting on the job!"

"Don't worry," he said firmly, "the job is yours." We shook hands. For a few seconds our eyes met, and we looked searchingly at each other. Once again I felt uncomfortable, and I turned abruptly and left.

Two weeks seemed an eternity; I spent a lot of it thinking and worrying about Szaja Spiegel and the job. Why had he picked me? What did he think of me? He was attractive in a terribly serious way. His gray suit had been in need of pressing, but then again there were no cleaners in the ghetto. For some reason, I wanted him to like me. Because of the job? I wondered. Certainly I needed the job—and the daily soup that came with it! But I was also curious about him. I wondered if he had a family, where he lived, what his background was. I was surprised at myself. Why all this curiosity? Why was he suddenly on my mind?

When the day finally arrived, I dressed carefully and rushed to his office, filled more with fear than hope at the prospect of confronting Szaja Spiegel.

He smiled. In his quiet, deliberate way, he seemed pleased to see me. He led me to a desk stacked high with documents printed in German.

"These coal ration sheets will be arriving in great quantities from the Reich. They are for the cities of Berlin, Essen, Düsseldorf, etc. We have been ordered to log them, complete them, and compute the coal ration on a per-family basis. Complete and file whatever you can but only translate what is absolutely necessary. After we are finished with them, they will be sent back to Germany."

It all sounded well organized and so typically German. But it would keep me as well as several hundred others busy for many months to come. Most importantly, there was the noontime soup; although devoid of any nourishment, the watery, hot lunch was better than nothing at all.

For some time, Szaja did not speak to me unless it concerned one of the work projects. But I often caught him staring at me, seemingly lost in thought. Why was he staring? I wondered. Was it about my work? Or was there another reason? I was confused. I very much wanted to talk to him on a personal level, to find out about him, but I did not know how to begin. I remained curious yet reserved, sensing, finally, that his stares did indeed represent more than just an interest in my work.

One day about three weeks after I had started working for him, he slowly approached my desk and asked if he could walk me home that evening. I nodded, hoping that I would finally get a chance to ask the questions that had been nagging me.

"I want to thank you again for hiring me," I began as we started walking home, "but do you think the German forms will continue to arrive in the ghetto?"

He looked surprised at my question. "I hope for a long time," he answered. "We need the work to keep several hundred people busy. Don't worry, you won't be without a job in the near future." He seemed to have read my mind. "What kind of work did you do for Adolf Goetz?" Szaja wanted to know.

"Just some secretarial work—nothing exceptional, but it allowed me my midday soup."

"And before that?"

"Before that I had no work. But what about you? What did you do before the war?"

"I was a schoolteacher in a Jewish school, teaching teenagers Yiddish. In my spare time, I wrote prose and poetry. Some of my stories were published in a literary journal in Poland."

I had already heard this about Szaja, but I politely asked more questions until I could comfortably ask the one for which I really wanted an answer. "Why did you hire me?" I asked softly. "So many others were waiting for a job."

He looked thoughtful. "When I first saw you near the stove, I guessed you were seventeen, maybe eighteen. You were wearing a brown suit and a white blouse, neat, clean, slim, and your face, sort of oval, pale. I noticed you had just a touch of lipstick." He was silent for a moment, then continued, "Maybe the main reason I hired you was because of your large, green eyes. You looked so frightened and so sad and seemed so distant, almost in another world. If I were writing a poem, I would say, 'Your silence is the wall I cannot scale.' How's that?"

"It certainly sounds like poetry, not like a normal statement," I answered gingerly. A stinging wind was cutting across my cheeks, yet my face was hot and flushed. I was grateful for the darkness.

What Szaja had said was true. I was in my separate world and did not want to be reached. Everyone I loved had been taken away from me. I still felt too much pain for any new connections. Yet I also wanted someone to care, to notice. His continued glances seemed to follow me. I liked the attention, but I wondered what he expected of me. After all, he was twice my age, and I had long since given up hoping for a future, much less for love. In the ghetto, we had no control over our own destiny, and we lived only one day—sometimes only one minute—at a time. Surely this was no time to fall in love. I knew that I wanted him to care, to notice me. But was there more?

The other questions I had planned to ask were lost in my confusion, and nothing more was said. We arrived at my door, shook hands, and said good night.

But our little ritual had begun. Every evening thereafter, he waited for me downstairs at the entrance to the building where we worked, and we walked together through the silent streets. One evening, curiosity overcame my reserve, and I found the courage to ask about his family.

He hesitated for a long time before answering. "Well, I suppose I should tell you that I was married before the war. We had a child, little Eva, but she died in the ghetto. Now I live with my parents."

I was shocked as this reality hit me: I was seeing a married man! "What about your wife?" I asked cautiously.

"She also lives in the ghetto and shares a room with her father. Our love has been dead a long time. I do not see her, and the separation is legal. The divorce will follow."

A ghetto divorce? I couldn't help thinking that only Rumkowski could grant one of those.

I was even more troubled than before. Somehow it frightened me to be seeing a married man. What would Mother have said? I dared not think.

Then, one night in February, he asked me if I would stay after work. "Remember I told you that I write poetry and prose?" he asked. "Tonight I would like to read some of it to you, if you'd care to listen. It's written in Yiddish."

Despite my trepidation, I was excited and even a bit pleased that he had asked me to listen to his work, and I agreed.

We stayed at the office after everyone else had left, and Szaja began his reading. His characters came to life; even the animals in his tales were believable. His stories portrayed ghetto life with its sadness, its beauty, its gruesome deaths. While he read, Betczak, the janitor, swept the floor around us, muttering angrily under his breath, "What kind of crazy people work twelve hours and then stay, sitting in a cold room, bundled up in coats, hats, and scarves, reading foolish stories?"

"You are absolutely right," Szaja responded with a laugh. Patting Betczak on the shoulder, he continued his reading.

Our meetings began to assume a pattern: we worked from 8:00 to 8:00, Szaja would read until about 10:00, then we'd walk to my door hand in hand. Our tender moments were stolen, although not always private. We often embraced and kissed while the neighbors watched and walked around us. They looked disapprovingly at us; their harsh glances hurt.

My roommates, Ida and Gerda Rabinowicz, had already warned me, "People are talking. You're wasting your time with Szaja. He's still married, you know, and he's too old for you. Anyway, what does a married man want with a young girl? Think about it. You should put a stop to this now."

I listened and although I was shocked at their strong reaction, I did not defend myself. It was too late to change anything. I cared for Szaja, I was no longer completely alone, and I had begun to depend on seeing him, on being close to him.

One evening, while walking home, he handed me a paper scroll. "I wanted to bring you flowers," he said, "but there are no flowers in the ghetto. My words will have to do."

I looked at the sky with its bright, sparkling stars fastened to a cloudless, black sky. The frosty air left me breathless. We kissed for a long time, then said our good nights. I waited until I got upstairs and then slowly opened the scroll. Inside was a hand-written poem:

Eyes, your eyes are green—
two little springs framed with grasses.
In their shadow plays the warm evening gold
like above tall birch trees.
Eyes, your eyes are green,
two little springs brimming with drops of water.
There I lie in the evening amid the grasses
And small, green springs are singing at my head.
It's good to be alone in evening darkness,
to drink cool wine from your green eyes—
I, too, become a sad birch tree
bent trembling over little springs.

I read the poem over and over, feeling happy and sad at the same time.

I tried to thank Szaja the following day but could not find the right words. He gave me a melancholic smile. "If I made you happy, then that is my reward. I want you always to be happy. It matters a great deal to me."

But many concerns were standing in the way of my being happy. I was worried about Szaja's wife, the fact that he was married, his age, the war, and the ghetto. Moreover, I still did not know how I felt about him. Did I really love him? I wasn't sure. I knew that I needed his love and his attention, but what was I doubting? I did not want to lose him; I wanted life to continue as it was. Surely I was in love, yet there were nagging doubts.

The next morning at work, Szaja looked at my sopping shoes. "You're cold and wet, your shoes are soaked! Why didn't you tell me that you don't have proper shoes or boots?"

"You know it wouldn't have changed a thing," I answered. "You can't buy a new pair of shoes or boots."

But I was pleased that he'd noticed, that he cared. I thought of new shoes, but I had nothing to trade in the black market, and to barter for shoes, I would need a great deal of bread or some other kind of food.

That night, back in my room, I looked at my few belongings. There was a small suitcase we had brought from Hamburg, Mother's old coat, and a pair of high-heeled shoes. My eyes fell on her large, light brown leather hatbox. Would there be enough leather for a pair of boots? But this was my inheritance, my only link to the past. Would Mother want me to cut up her leather hatbox for boots? I was not sure. Finally, need overcame sentimentality, and I decided to take the box to work.

Szaja looked at the round hatbox. He immediately understood and was delighted. "A stroke of genius! I'll take you to the shoemaker after work, and we'll decide how to proceed."

"But this was my mother's legacy to me," I murmured.

"Your mother would have wanted you to have the boots. In times like these, we must do anything—anything—to help us survive."

After work we walked to the cobbler. He was bent over

his bench but looked up with interest when he saw the large, leather case. He was eager to make boots for me.

"The price?" I worried.

"No problem. I won't charge you if I can keep the leftovers, which will provide enough material for another pair of shoes. However, we do need lining fabric."

"Lining?"

"How about a piece of a blanket?" he suggested.

The next day, I brought him a quarter of a camel-hair blanket. He traced the outline of my foot on a piece of paper and promised to have the boots ready for a fitting in a week's time. Two weeks later, the boots were completed and were absolutely magnificent, beautiful and warm. March brought more snow, and our winter seemed never-ending. The boots kept my feet dry. Still, when I looked at them, I thought of Mother and how much I missed her.

Night after night Szaja and I continued our ritual walk from the office to my front door. We would kiss at the doorstep. It was not easy to part. Then I'd walk quickly upstairs so that I could look out the window at the lone, stooped figure of Szaja Spiegel as he walked away.

One evening, Szaja seemed to have something on his mind. His fingers, hidden in woolen gloves, held my arm tightly. "If your mother were alive"—he hesitated—"I'd ask her for permission to marry you. She'd agree, I'm sure!"

I was stunned. Was this a statement or a proposal? Mother had been dead almost eight months now; still, I knew what she would have said. I could almost hear her voice: "No, never, you're just eighteen. This is not the match I have dreamed of for you. This man is thirty-eight years old, separated, not yet divorced..." She would have been furious.

"Well?" Szaja wanted to know.

I could not bring myself to tell him how much Mother would have disapproved of him, of me, of our relationship. Instead, I answered, "Mother is dead—she cannot reply. But what about your divorce? It is so complicated in the ghetto."

"My divorce could be arranged."

We walked in silence. I thought about a ghetto marriage with its constant hunger and pain. And what about children? Certainly I would not want to bring children into this world! Anyway, it was not likely that there could be any. Women in the ghetto no longer menstruated; poor nutrition had put a stop to that. For the same reason, men suffered impotence. I looked at Szaja's face, a million questions plaguing me at once.

He understood. "Look, perhaps it is a crazy notion to think of marriage here and now. But I have another suggestion. There is a small room I could obtain from the housing office. It is on Ribna Street. It could be our room, yours and mine . . ."

I shook my head. "I couldn't. It's not proper. It isn't done." The thought of being alone with Szaja both excited and frightened me. I did love him and wanted a closer relationship, but for me there were too many obstacles. In spite of his words, his reassurances that he loved me, I was still skeptical, still worried, still confused. I was certain about only one thing: such an arrangement would lead to ugly rumors and scandal.

Szaja tried to console and convince me at the same time. "You could live there alone. I would come and stay just a few hours and then at night go back to my parents. Won't you reconsider? Please . . ."

"No!" I shook my head, unable to say more.

"All right, then," he said, "let's continue as is. But will you promise me not to see anyone else, not to talk to anyone else? I am terribly jealous."

It was the first time that he had confessed to being possessive—and I was happy to be possessed. "I promise. I will see no one else. It will be just you and me. And after the war . . . ?"

"I have so many plans," he interrupted. "After the war, I will be well known, and you'll be my wife, and life will be very different from anything you can imagine now. Life will be good!"

For a moment, there seemed to be something to look forward to, some faint glimmer of love and a normal life after the war.

Meanwhile, the reality of our existence was taking its toll. Conversation at the office revolved around two topics: the feared German "Aussiedlungen," in which they rounded up groups of people and sent them out of the ghetto; and food—the lack of food, the growing hunger, the forthcoming rations, food before the war, food after the war, and most of all, the dream of a full stomach. Would that time ever come?

During one such conversation about bread, Szaja suddenly burst out, "Promise me never to talk about food or hunger. It is vulgar and degrading." And I agreed, but not talking about food hardly erased it from Szaja's mind or mine. Whether we were awake or asleep, our visions, our dreams, and our thoughts revolved constantly around food and eating, the smell and taste of bread.

Ironically, barely three weeks after his outburst, Szaja was sent to work in a bakery. Although this assignment was only temporary, it was considered a special reward from our boss, Henryk Neftalin. Now Szaja could eat as much bread as he desired. I was happy for him, but my own hunger remained as painful as ever. I hoped that he would bring me a slice of his bread. He never did. I struggled to understand, but I was hurt, disappointed, and often very angry. Not even one slice of bread for someone you love? I thought him selfish and uncaring. Yet I was afraid to lose him, so I said nothing.

One day, while Szaja was still working in the bakery, my friend Elli stopped at my desk. "Celia, I want to talk to you about Szaja."

"I'd rather not discuss it," I answered.

"We are friends, and it is important to let you know what I think and what people are saying."

"I really don't care what anyone else says!" I replied defensively.

"He is conceited, selfish, and he's too old—and still married, too!" Elli was angry now and very direct.

"And you?" I lashed out. "You meet your German Wacht-meister wherever he is stationed for his two-hour guard duty. You even stayed with him in his guardhouse on Baluter Ring. Why? For a loaf of bread? You cannot possibly care for a German who keeps his gun loaded against us."

As soon as the harsh words had escaped my lips, I was sorry. But it was too late. Elli looked crushed. "I will not defend myself. You do what you think is right, and so will I. We won't discuss this matter again."

We embraced, we remained friends, but now there was a silent rift between us. Elli had confirmed what I had begun to suspect about Szaja but had not wanted to admit. I could explain away my earlier doubts, but Szaja's selfishness—that I could never forget!

The spring of 1943 was mild and made our misery easier to bear. I was sure now, despite everything I knew, that I was in love with Szaja. On late evenings, we stopped in the courtyard next to my house and stood on the old wooden cover of the dry well. I would be lost in Szaja's embrace, my head resting on his shoulder, warmed by his arms hidden in the sleeves of my jacket. I was happy and momentarily at peace.

In July, Henryk Neftalin called me into the administrative offices. "You have been transferred and will be working for Dr. Oskar Singer, director of archives in the Statistical Department on Plac Koscielny."

Stunned into silence, I could barely hold back my tears. "Why?" I finally managed to ask.

"You know German and will have no problems with the writing and spelling of the daily reports. I thought you'd be pleased." His voice sounded matter-of-fact; it left no room for discussion.

"When?" I asked.

"Day after tomorrow."

The thought of leaving Szaja and going to work at the other end of town filled me with unhappiness. I confided my fears to him. A few days later, he told me he had a surprise.

"You don't have to worry about our spending time together. I'll still be able to see you every evening. In fact, I've arranged it so that we'll be working together, as before, right here at Rybna 8. You'll leave the Statistical Department at 6:00 P.M. and walk back over the wooden bridge to Rybna Street. I'll be waiting for you. Then we'll work together from

6:00 to 8:00. You'll have two jobs instead of one. Neftalin has promised."

I was pleased, but I wondered why he hadn't asked me first.

"And now I have another surprise for you. On Sunday evening, there will be a concert in a private room. I have been asked to attend, and I want to take you with me."

"A concert in 1943, in the ghetto?"

He nodded. "They will play chamber music and perform two of my lullabies. I wrote the words; someone else composed the music."

I was excited and could hardly wait.

That Sunday, Szaja picked me up at 7:00, and we walked to an old, dilapidated building on Marynarska Street. The audience sat on the floor against the walls and chatted noisily until they noticed Szaja. A hush fell over the room. Obviously, they knew him and were curious. We took our places on the floor and waited. The room was gray and dismal. Four musicians, seated on chairs in the center of the room, were tuning their instruments.

The audience became very quiet, and someone announced, "We'll start with two lullabies by Szaja Spiegel. Please keep your applause silent in order to avoid unnecessary noise."

A young woman stepped forward, looked toward the musicians, and they began to play. Her beautiful soprano voice produced vibrating melodies for Szaja's haunting words. The applause was a thunderous, silent clapping of hands. The musicians continued with various pieces of chamber music.

The sound of their music reminded me of the last concert I had attended with my parents. That was in 1938, when they had taken me to the Curio Haus to listen to a piano recital. Afterward, we had gone to a nearby Konditorei (an elegant coffee shop) for ice cream. We had not gotten home until after 11:00. I had felt very grown-up and happy then—a lifetime ago. Tears, long repressed, now streamed down my face.

The musicians played until exhausted, then packed their instruments away. It was almost midnight when someone with an accordion began to play a tango. Several couples danced. Szaja took my hand and put his arm around my waist. He was a surprisingly good dancer; I had not expected that this serious, introspective man would even step onto a dance floor, so I was quite pleased. He held me tightly, and we danced until the music stopped. Even then, no one made a move to leave. We reassumed our seats on the floor and stayed until early morning, when everyone left and quietly dispersed throughout the ghetto. I was sad to see this wonderful, happy occasion come to an end.

That summer, we walked twice to Marysin at the end of the ghetto, the only countrylike green spot within the ghetto's confines. On one occasion, we saw Chaim Rumkowski in his droshky as it came rushing past us. He was well dressed, well fed, and seemingly without a care in the world. Most of us feared and detested him, although sometimes we thought of him with envy. He seemed to suffer none of the deprivations we did. He didn't know the pain of hunger and cold. Even his horse and driver were well fed. He was responsible to the Germans for the entire ghetto, and it often seemed to us that he was more on their side than ours. All orders issued by the Germans appeared in ghetto posters over his name and signature, and his temper and power were said to be awesome.

"Szaja," I said, "although this is hardly a possibility, if I were ever to meet him face to face, I would ask for food, only food."

Szaja looked at me aghast. "You'd be playing with fire. Rumkowski is a pig. I don't even consider him a human being. Two years ago, before you arrived in the ghetto, I wrote a song about a small infant in a crib, the father scrounging for food to feed his family and not succeeding. Rumkowski heard about it and thought it was an insult. He threatened me and created a ruling that outlawed my writing. It was only with the intervention of Henryk Neftalin that he agreed to leave me alone. I in turn promised to ignore him in my poetry and prose. But aside from that he is also known as a womanizer—in spite of the fact that he is supposedly impotent."

I was shocked but still curious about this powerful man.

Only too soon, summer turned into fall, which was just as quickly replaced by winter. It was cruelly cold; every day the water in the washbucket was hidden beneath a sheet of ice. Walking to work at Plac Koscielny was difficult. Icy, knife-sharp winds carried snow and sleet that seeped mercilessly through every crevice of my now-worn boots, numbing my toes until they no longer seemed a part of me. The painful grip of hunger was relentless, as food rations were in even shorter supply than in the past.

Hunger prevented sleep. One morning, my empty, growling stomach awakened me shortly before 5:00 A.M. I got out of bed, threw a blanket around my shoulders, and looked out of the window into the still, dark sky. The windowpanes were covered with icy glistening stars. I traced the delicate patterns for some moments. It was peaceful. The war, hunger, and desperation were momentarily forgotten, replaced by the morning's beauty. Dancing snowflakes threw themselves against the panes, demanding entry, then slowly, flake by flake, settled quietly on the window ledge. The snow lay glistening on the ground, innocent and sparkling. Layer upon layer of fresh, sticky flakes had grown overnight to almost three feet in height. I remembered snowball fights, sleigh rides, skiing in the mountains, and the fun and laughter of years past.

Suddenly there was an urgent knock on the door, and a man's voice bellowed impatiently, "It's urgent, I need to talk to you!"

As I opened the door, the neighbors, roused by the noise, peered cautiously out of their rooms. Outside stood a "Sonder," a member of the Jewish Special Police Force. I noticed with relief that he was one of ours and not a German. He was tall, blue-eyed, and very young.

"Are you Cecilia Landau?" he demanded.

I nodded reluctantly.

"You have been summoned. Hurry! Dress and come with me." I stopped breathing for a second. He, too, looked frightened.

"I—summoned? Where?"

"The Kripo, Kriminalpolizei," he whispered. This word was always said in whispers, perhaps because it meant a visit to Criminal Police headquarters where, rumor had it, many had been killed and tortured.

"Why?" I asked, my voice trembling.

The Sonder looked annoyed and impatient. "I don't know; I was only told to bring you. Please hurry, it is dangerous to keep the Germans waiting."

The thought of the little red house on Koscielna Street made my head swim. This was the house we always kept away from, the street we never used. Many had been taken there. Few returned. Without warning, the muscles of my empty stomach contracted into one continuous, painful cramp. Fear settled there and refused to leave.

"God, what have I done?"

"I don't know. I'm just ordered to bring you. Will you please hurry? If we delay, it will only be worse."

"Worse? It's bad then?"

The Sonder did not reply. Szaja's name popped into my mind. Would he wonder and worry if I didn't appear for work? I had no way of letting him know, of telling him that I had been summoned. What if I disappeared? He'd never know where or how.

The Sonder stepped impatiently from one foot to the other. I rushed to put on my coat and scarf.

It was shortly after 5:30 when we left. The ghetto was very quiet, and we did not encounter a soul. We walked along in silence, hearing only the snow crackling under our soles. In spite of the shivering cold, my skin was sticky and crawling with perspiration. Why me? Why had they found me? They did not keep records of our names and addresses. Out of a hundred thousand people in the ghetto, why would they summon an eighteen-year-old girl of no importance to anyone?

I thought again about the house on Koscielna Street. What would they do to me? I dared not guess.

We finally stopped in front of the building and slowly climbed the steps to the front door. The Sonder opened it, hurriedly called out my name, turned, and ran. He was gone by the time I closed the creaking door behind me. The room was dark, lit only by a small lamp, and smelled of stale cooking odors and cigarette smoke. At least it was warm. I stared with envy at the green tile stove in the corner. A German entered. I waited in watchful silence as he walked arrogantly across the room. Even indoors, he wore a black velour hat and a black leather coat that matched his freshly shined black boots. His face was red and well fed. Icy cold, steel-gray eyes stared out at me from under the hat. I stood straight, facing the German. I wanted to cry but dared not. I thought of those who had been beaten to death here, those who had been sentenced here and hanged on gallows in Bazarny Rynek. Simple execution was not enough for the Germans; death had to be a show of power, a warning. We would frequently be rounded up and herded at gunpoint into the square to witness SS justice. The bodies were often left hanging for days. From my office window, I could see them swaying back and forth in the wind, throwing long shadows on the ground. The memory made me shudder.

"Your name?"

"Cecilia Landau," I replied.

"I know that you have a radio and contact with the outside. A reliable source told me." He sounded matter-of-fact.

A radio? A reliable source? I was stunned. I knew the ghetto had informers, men who made a living and received food bonuses by denouncing their neighbors to the Germans. As a result, one man had been shot for smuggling food from the Aryan side; another was hung when a radio was found hidden in his room. But why would anyone inform on me?

I shook my head.

"Well, speak up!" he yelled.

"I don't have a radio, and I do not have contact with the world outside."

"I know you do—why do you bother to lie?"

"I'm telling the truth, please believe me," I pleaded.

"I know you are lying!" he said with a hoarse laugh.

With a sudden motion, his right arm jerked upward, and his fist flew toward me, hitting the left side of my head with a strong, ringing impact. I reeled to one side. Shock numbed the immediate pain, but a muted throbbing pulsated behind my hot and bruised face. Awkwardly, I straightened up, but the ache on the left side of my head made looking at the German difficult.

"You know that I will beat an admission out of you. Why not save yourself more pain?"

"But I do not have a radio!" I desperately replied.

His fist shot toward me, hitting the left side of my head and face over and over again. Blood rushed into my mouth, leaving a warm, sticky taste; then it ran slowly down my beige coat. Dull noises began to fill my head; there were a thousand popping sounds in my left ear. Suddenly, a violent sound roared through both my ears and exploded into an eerie silence. My sight was blurred, and the room was spinning. He wanted an admission—he wanted to know where the radio was. Should I say yes, even though I didn't own a radio? I could not possibly produce a radio! This was madness! It couldn't be happening!

"How about the radio? I'm losing patience with you!"

He waved a revolver in my face. Pain enveloped my head like a heavy curtain. I could barely see. My eyes were heavy, the skin around them thick and swollen. Still he kept hitting my face. My legs trembled and threatened to give way. The German's voice seemed to come from some distant world. My mumbled replies had become incoherent, but I made one last effort.

"Radio? There's no radio. My room—no radio!"

His laughter was piercing, his words muffled, and his figure hazy. His huge fist hit me again and again. Then, as suddenly as the beating had begun, it ended. His shouts stopped, and the room was filled with an awful silence. I hoped that he had gotten bored, his violence and hate spent for the moment. With a sudden motion, his strong hands pressed against my back; he pushed me toward the door, opened it, and shoved me outside and down the stairs. I fell into a white, wet blanket of snow, leaving blotches of red blood on the diamond flakes.

The German stood in the open door, laughing. "A jealous woman must have denounced you!" he screamed.

My thoughts were scrambled and confused, my mind unable and unwilling to comprehend what had happened. The cold snow and the piercing wind gave momentary relief to the pain, and I tried to concentrate on how lucky I was to be alive. I knew I had to get up and get away. If only Szaja were there to help me... But I was alone. Crawling and walking, every step filled with pain, I managed to drag myself from the street.

It was daylight now, and the ghetto was bustling with activity. But where were the noises that should go with all the bustling? They were dim and seemed to come from a great distance. Slowly, carefully, I turned my head from side to side. Sounds came clearly through the right ear, but through the left—nothing! The beating—how much damage? Maybe it was permanent? I told myself that it was temporary, that it would improve, that the ear would heal.

Workers hurrying to their jobs looked at me but did not stop. They had seen this before. On hands and knees, I reached my building and somehow dragged myself up the concrete stairs to the third floor. I managed to find my keys in my pocket, but they were useless. The keyhole eluded my focus. After minutes of grappling and scratching, key against lock, the door opened. A note from Szaja under the door? No—there was nothing. He had not looked for me.

I fell onto my bed. The pillow and sheets were soon stained with blood. The throbbing in my left ear was deafening. I wondered if someone had actually denounced me or if I was just a random victim of yet another SS strategy. For the moment, I put such thoughts out of my mind. I was alive; I had survived! Gratefully, I watched each curling, steamy cloud of breath rise in the frigid air above my bed.

The next morning, I went back to work. The bruises on my face could not be hidden. Everyone noticed; no one dared ask. Even Szaja pretended that all was normal, that nothing had happened. But I knew that the ghetto grapevine had reached the office and that all knew of my visit to the Kripo and the subsequent beating. Even though it was too painful to talk about, I was hurt—I desperately wanted and needed sympathy. None was forthcoming.

One afternoon a few days later, I felt a hand resting gently on my shoulder. Without turning, I knew it was Szaja's, and for that one moment I was at peace. He understood. I could feel his silent compassion, his love, and his worry about me. He must have known what had happened, but his silence made it clear that he would never ask. He tapped gently on my shoulder, and I turned toward him. Even the thick, black-rimmed glasses could not hide the sadness and pity in his brown eyes.

"I've been talking to you, but you didn't hear me! Unless you look at my face or my lips, you don't react! I'm worried."

I shrugged, but I was shocked that the compensations I had been making for my lack of hearing had been so obvious that he had noticed. For the past week, I had made it a habit to turn my head so my right ear was toward the speaker. I had also begun to read lips.

"Please do me a favor," pleaded Szaja, "see Dr. Kronenberg. I've known her since childhood. She is good and she is understanding. She'll see you this afternoon, she has promised me. Do go—just to please me? The pain in your eyes is staring back at me, and then suddenly you retreat to a far, dark place in your mind."

For Szaja's sake, I agreed to go. But I realized that my own reluctance stemmed from a fear of finding out that my hearing loss was permanent.

Szaja handed me a slip of paper on which he had written the doctor's address, and I left the office shortly after 6:00 P.M. I found the building without too much trouble. The courtyard was deserted, the structure gray and in disrepair like all ghetto dwellings, the stairway unlit and filthy. On the second floor at the end of the hallway was a door with a nameplate that read, "Kronenberg."

The tiny room was filled with waiting patients. They sat silently in semidarkness, and I joined them. I looked at the tall, still young man with the bandaged hand, the ten- or twelve-year-old girl with a bundled infant in her arms, the older woman with hollow eyes and sallow skin, and the lit- tle man with a snow-white beard. He wore slippers and held onto a cane. For a moment they all watched me, the new- comer, but when I sat down to wait with them, they lost interest.

It was a long, tedious wait; more than once I was tempted to get up and leave. Yet I stayed. Now I had to know. It was evening before I got to see Dr. Kronenberg.

She was a small, thin woman; her gray hair was arranged in a heavy braid and pinned to the top of her head. I guessed that she was in her fifties. The ghetto years had not been kind to her. She had pale, piercing eyes, and her movements were quick and impatient.

"What can I do for you?" she asked abruptly.

"I have trouble hearing with the left ear."

She nodded, and without a word she proceeded with her examination, using strange, tubelike instruments. Occasion- ally she would hit a tuning fork against her knee and then hold it next to my left ear.

"Did the sounds reach you?" she wanted to know.

I shook my head.

When she checked the right ear, I could hear everything. She put the instruments on the table beside her and sat down on a small stool facing me. Neither one of us spoke. Several minutes passed before she finally asked, "A beating?"

"Yes." My reply was curt.

Her fingers gently traced the welts, scabs, and bruises on the left side of my face. "When?"

"A week ago!" I replied.

She sat in thoughtful silence.

"I'm sorry, but I cannot help," she said sadly. "You will

have to adjust and make do with one good ear. The ghetto medical facilities are horrible at best. You know that. Maybe, just maybe, after the war something can be done to restore your hearing. I'm not sure."

I started to cry, short, choking, angry sobs. Silently, Dr. Kronenberg sat and waited until I calmed down. There was nothing else to say. We shook hands, and I handed her a ghetto twenty-mark bill; it was all I had left.

Adjust—it sounded simple but somehow not so simple. Still, I was lucky to be alive. I could only hope and pray and take one day at a time.

In spite of the late hour, Szaja was still waiting for me at the office. He looked at my tearstained face but didn't ask any questions. I was grateful. He gently kissed the left side of my head. I could feel his tears on my hair. He turned and walked out of the office, closing the door quietly. Somehow he knew that I needed to be alone.

Much later, when I had calmed down, I began to walk home. I sensed that I was being followed, even before I heard the steady, persistent clicking of footsteps behind me. As I turned, my pursuer came to an abrupt halt, and we stood facing each other. I breathed a sigh of relief. She was only a small woman, probably in her late thirties. She was wearing a black, shabby coat that hung loosely on her thin body. Her reddish-blond hair was pulled back with a large metal clip, and her gray eyes looked out of a tired, drawn face. She stood stark still and stared at me.

"You are Cecilia Landau?" she asked in an angry voice.

"Yes, but how do you know? Who are you?"

"Rena, Szaja's wife."

Szaja's wife! The words exploded in my head. Although I

knew that she existed, Szaja had stubbornly refused to give me any more information about her than he had on our first walk home. Now here she was, scrutinizing every inch of my face and body. Her stunted shadow lay at her feet in the moonlight.

In an agitated voice, she sputtered, "I want you to keep away from Szaja! Stop seeing him! If you don't, I'll go to the Kripo and give them your name!"

"The Kripo?" I whispered. "Give them my name?"

Suddenly it all fit. I remembered the German's words as he threw me out the door: "A jealous woman must have turned you in!"

"You, you turned me in?" I shouted. "You did this? What kind of a human being does that—and to another Jew? And now you threaten me again?"

Blinded by my fury, I could not look at her. How could she? My anger was greater than any I had ever known. As I looked at her face, contorted with hatred and vengeance, I, too, was so full of hatred that I felt capable of murder. I knew I would never forgive her for what she had done. I couldn't bear to look at her; I turned and ran.

That night I lay awake trying to decide what to do. Should I tell Szaja? Did he already know? Perhaps she had told him and threatened him, too. Should I continue seeing him? Would she turn me in again? Was my love for Szaja so important that I would risk my life?

After a sleepless night of questioning myself over and over, I decided not to tell Szaja about the confrontation and to continue seeing him. I had so few friends left, I reasoned. I was fully aware of what I was risking, but I needed Szaja, his love, his companionship, his closeness, his attention.

If Szaja sensed my turmoil in the days that followed, he kept silent, and I dared not broach the subject. Once again, I was afraid of losing him.

The following week, Rumkowski came to inspect our office. I was scared of this temperamental man. Throughout his inspection, I worried that he might send me to a factory to do hard physical labor. But Elli and I, as well as about fifty other young women, were lucky. We were singled out to work in the newly formed workers' evening kitchen. I was to work in the office; the other girls were to be waitresses. In addition to our daily soup, we would receive a supplemental plate with a little meat, vegetable, and half a potato—a banquet!

I couldn't wait to tell Szaja. But instead of being happy for me, he was very angry. Once again he launched into his tirade against Rumkowski: "I hate the thought of you working for this pig. I told you before, he's no good. Watch yourself!"

There was hatred in Szaja's eyes. But we both knew that there was no way to decline the offer.

"We'll have a little more food!" I reminded him, trying to get him out of his angry mood.

"Just be careful, very careful. He's a pig, a child molester, and a lecher!"

As soon as I could, I began bringing the small cutlet of ground horse meat from my dinner to Szaja when he picked me up in the evening. Hungrily, he would wolf down the meat, which I had carefully wrapped in paper. He never offered a word of thanks. Hunger, I rationalized, excused his crudeness. Still, I wondered.

A short while after I started working in the kitchen, I began to understand Szaja's warning about Rumkowski. Every evening, he came to inspect our work. Some he praised, some he scolded, and those who displeased him he beat with his cane. One evening while I was working alone in the office, Rumkowski entered, pulled up a chair, and sat down.

"Do you have family in Palestine?"

"My father's two brothers," I replied.

"I want your promise," he continued. "After the war, you have to ask them to help me."

I was confused. Rumkowski needing help? Why was he worried about the future? Was it fear of possible revenge from his fellow Jews or fear of the Germans?

The following evening, he sat down again next to my desk. "I want you to move," he said sharply. "There is a nice room above the kitchen, and I will be able to come see you there."

Once again Szaja's warning came to mind, and I started to cry. "Please, let me stay where I am, please, please . . ."

His cane came down brutally on my shoulder. "After all I have done for you, how dare you refuse?" he yelled furiously.

Luck was on my side: three days later, the kitchens were closed on orders from the Germans. Food supplies were exhausted, and Elli and I were reassigned to work in the saddlery.

The walk to the saddlery was a long one, and the return in the evening exhausting. Every evening, I looked forward to Szaja's company. Then, one evening, without warning, he didn't appear. The next night I waited again but was again disappointed. Night after night for the next few weeks I still waited and hoped. He did not appear. Our ritual, started months earlier, had ended.

I was constantly in tears, but I did not try to see him. I feared his estranged wife and what she might do to me. I tried to convince myself that it was better this way, even though my loneliness was almost unbearable. The days and weeks passed, and I was still in pain, still wondering why Szaja had stopped seeing me. Did he no longer love me? Had he never loved me? Was it because of my working for Rumkowski, or was he frightened of his wife's possible retaliation? I had no answers. The only certainty was the unmerciful life of the ghetto.

It was the beginning of a new year—1944. Elli and I were on our way to work when we stopped, as usual, to look at the dreaded deportation lists posted on walls throughout the ghetto: "The following persons are to report within thirty-six hours for resettlement to another camp." Under the column for the L's was "Cecilia Landau." Panic-stricken, I grabbed Elli's arm.

"My name, Elli, my name is on the list! Why me? I don't want to leave—I want to stay here," I cried. "I'm afraid of leaving. What shall I do? Here I know the horrors; someplace else I will be among strangers and totally alone to face new horrors. I want to stay. I'm so scared . . ." My voice cracked.

"The only thing we can do is try to find someone who has connections," Elli answered.

Although I couldn't bring myself to face Szaja, I knew that he was really my only hope.

Elli seemed to be reading my mind. "Maybe Szaja?" she said. "This evening, after work, I'll go and talk to him. He knows everyone in the ghetto and maybe he'd be willing to help."

I nodded, but without much hope.

I knew that for the next eight hours while we were at

work, Elli couldn't contact anyone—precious time wasted. That evening, I checked the lists again, hoping there had been an error, but my name was still there. That night, I lay awake in bed, trying to think of ways to remain in the ghetto, but there was no chance without help from someone with influence. In the morning, I rushed to meet Elli at the wooden bridge.

"I spoke with Szaja last night," she began, "and told him about your deportation. He only said that he'd try. But no promises."

We walked in silence to the next corner and checked the posted lists again—still no change. The hours at work crawled slowly. I prayed, I hoped, and I cried. At lunchtime, I checked the lists again—no change. I had eight hours left. I knew that if I did not appear at the station, the police would come and pick me up. I had never known such desperation. That evening, we hastily left the saddlery and rushed once more to check the lists. Quickly, I ran my finger down the L's—no Landau! I couldn't believe it. I checked a second time: my name had indeed been deleted. I took a few slow, deep breaths, relieved but totally exhausted.

The following evening after work, I stopped at Szaja's office. He seemed surprised to see me. "I want to thank you for your help," I said. "I'll always remember what you did for me—always."

He looked at me but said nothing. We shook hands, much like the day we first met, yet not at all like that first day. I wondered what had happened to our love, our friendship, but he offered no explanation. I left the office, grateful but very sad.

Weeks later, rumors drifted back that everyone on that

resettlement train had been killed. Szaja's gift to me—my life. But I was often disturbed by the thought that perhaps someone else's life had been taken in place of mine.

Eight months later, in August of 1944, the ghetto liquidation orders came. The Germans began closing off street after street with barricades so that we no longer had access to our rooms. Some people tried to hide, but they were flushed out by the Germans. For me, it no longer mattered. Just before they got to Pawia Street, I packed my small satchel and walked to the trains. Row upon row of filthy cattle cars were waiting for us. We didn't know where they were taking us, and I gave it very little thought. My thoughts were with Szaja. Where was he now? I wondered. Would he also have to leave the ghetto? Would we ever meet again?

Auschwitz ∾

1944

The room was filled
with mountains of hair,
blond, brown, and black,
curly, wavy, and straight.
Cold bare scalps—
who had ever heard
of women
without hair?
Their shining strands
left behind.
What will they do
with these mountains of hair?
"Fill pillows,
mattresses,
and chairs!"
Does it bother those
who use
these pillow and chairs
filled with human hair,
drenched with
blood,
with tears,
and with curses?

After almost three nightmarish years in the Lodz ghetto, I once again faced the unknown. By now, Elli and I had become good friends. We sat huddled together, quiet, apprehensive, wondering where we were going and what awaited us beyond the darkness of the train's locked doors.

Four long days in the vile-smelling cattle cars with their constant stops and starts ended when the mud-spattered train came to an abrupt halt. My watch showed 4:00 A.M. The early morning silence was broken by the shouts of Germans, the hard metallic sounds of clicking heels, and the angry scratching of barking dogs against the outside of the wooden cattle cars.

Suddenly, the doors were thrust open. The dark sky was lit up by the platform's huge, bright spotlights. I blinked my eyes, trying to adjust after four days of total darkness to the eerie, bright-yellow glow outside. Loudly amplified commands assaulted our ears.

"Raus, schnell, hurry, line up!"

There was a frightening urgency to these German commands, and we hurriedly climbed out of the cars. Elli and I stood side by side, two awkward teenagers.

"Where are we, what is this place?" I whispered.

A young, gaunt-looking man in blue-and-gray-striped pants and a matching long shirt and cap overheard us. The red armband on his sleeve read "Kapo." His sunken eyes looked at us incredulously. "Auschwitz! This is Auschwitz! You mean to tell me that you've never heard of this place?" He spoke in Polish.

We shook our heads. "Who are you, what is a Kapo?" Elli asked.

"Camp police, but I'm a prisoner and a Jew like you!" he replied.

"No one in the Lodz ghetto ever heard of this place," whispered Elli.

"Unbelievable—and I have been here almost two years! Do you know anyone named Luba? I'm looking for my sister. Could she have come with you?"

"Luba? We do not know a Luba, but you might ask around."

As the Germans in their clean and well-pressed SS uniforms approached us, the Kapo turned and ran. There must have been a thousand of us, stunned and milling about. Youngsters cried. Bewildered parents held them close and whispered soft words to comfort them. The Germans, impatient for some semblance of order, used their rifle butts to push and shove the mass of human bodies until they had us lined up five abreast.

"Men to the right, women to the left!" shouted a voice. Everyone moved slowly, reluctantly. Husbands and wives, sisters and brothers, parents and children, terrified at the thought of separation, held onto each other desperately. But quickly and without mercy, rifle butts came crashing down on tightly clasped fingers. There were no good-byes, only screams and broken, bleeding hands. Elli and I were pushed to the left, her father and older brother to the right. Already they were being herded away with the others. "What's happening? Where are they going?" Elli whispered.

I shook my head. Everything was happening so fast that we could not yet discern any pattern or meaning.

"Women, step forward," the German continued. "You to the right, you to the left!"

It soon became apparent that the older women and children were being separated from the rest of us, the stronger and younger ones. I looked at my watch: 4:10. Only minutes had passed since we'd left the trains. Life and death decided within seconds—at the whim of the German SS! My mind was in turmoil. What now, what next? Confused, I watched those around me. Some stood in stony silence, bewildered; others cried; some murmured almost inaudible sounds and whimpers

"Drop your bags, you'll get them later!" yelled the German in front of us.

Elli dropped her bag immediately, but I was determined to hold onto mine. It held my passport and the only documents that testified to the existence of my physical identity: "Cecilia Landau." Elli tore the bag from my hand and dropped it.

"You just saved yourself a beating!" screamed the German. "Column march!"

We stepped forward, following those in front of us, and were pushed toward a huge, low barracks, then herded inside.

"Undress completely! Fold your clothing neatly. Remove all jewelry, put it on the floor in front of you, and walk over to the left. Remember, I said ALL JEWELRY!" The voice in back of us was loud and threatening.

We did as we were told. Naked, we stood and waited, shivering in the sweltering room.

For the first time, I noticed our surroundings. The area was windowless but brightly lit. The light walls reflected the shadows of a jumble of human shapes. The putrid, suffocating odor of sweaty bodies hung in the air. Voices of male and female SS guards continued to shout commands. Sometimes they seemed to share a private joke and laughed raucously and ominously, their voices ringing with contempt. I felt a fear I had never known before.

We stood there like a covey of frightened birds. Not a word escaped our lips. We sensed some as yet unknown horror, but we kept our thoughts to ourselves. Elli's hand, damp and sticky, grasped mine, her nails digging into my flesh. We held each other's fear in our trembling hands. My eyes looked straight ahead, and my heart pounded violently so that I was unable to swallow.

The Kapo next to us, a dark-haired woman of about thirty, mumbled in a low voice, "They used to tattoo new arrivals with numbers." She pointed to her left arm, showing us six blue numbers prefixed with an A. "Now, instead, we shave your heads." She sounded tired and indifferent.

"Shave our heads?" Elli asked, incredulous. "Why? Why numbers?"

The Kapo was silent.

"Please, can't I keep my hair?" Elli pleaded in a tearful voice.

The Kapo looked at us with impatience and disgust. "In this place, you take what you get—if you get anything! You've got a lot to learn!" Angrily she turned and walked away. Elli's eyes looked glassy, and I could see tears gathering on the reddened lids.

There was a sudden commotion. The Germans yanked several women out of line.

"Stand straight!" they shouted. "Kapos, clip the hair!"

The Kapos obeyed, holding the hair taut in the left hand

while the right held the clippers. We watched in horror, knowing that the same awaited us. The clippers did their work well, traveling up and down the heads until nothing but bare scalps remained. Elli looked at me and asked in a barely audible whisper, "And after that?"

There was no time to answer before she was pulled away. Seconds later, I saw her black curls fall to the ground; minutes later, she was no longer the Elli I knew. I could barely recognize her. Her head was a round, white ball from which glazed brown eyes stared out at me. My own eyes filled with tears, but before I could cry, my arm was pinched savagely, and a heavyset SS woman pushed me forward. The Kapo next to her pulled my long, brown hair upward and proceeded to shave, running the clippers from the nape of my neck to the top of my head, onto the forehead and back again, repeating the motion several times until my hair slid past my naked shoulders and onto the floor. Bits and pieces covered my feet and stuck to my damp toes. I stared at the brown curls, then at the SS woman.

She was obese, stuffed into a uniform several sizes too small for her ample body. She was about thirty five years old, with frizzy blond hair, not even five feet tall. Her squinty eyes were hidden behind thick, rimless glasses. She laughed, enjoying every minute of our degradation. Pure hatred mixed with fear and pain swirled in my brain until I silently screamed and swore revenge.

As if reading my thoughts, the SS woman slapped my face hard with the back of her hand. My head reeled back, but the Kapo kept on clipping. As she shaved my armpits and all other body hair, I concentrated on my hatred: hatred for her, hatred for the Germans who had reduced me to this sweating, naked creature, without hair, without dignity. I was no longer a human being to them, just an expendable Jew. I remembered my father and sister: had they been brought to a place like this to endure a similar degradation—or, as in the case of my father, to be murdered? Would I ever know? I wanted to scream, to kick, to scratch. Instead, I stood in silent rage.

I looked at the mountains of hair around us, hair of every conceivable color. What would they do with all this hair? For several minutes, we stood motionless, then felt the hands of the Kapo pushing us toward the swinging doors. I was startled by a reflection in the upper glass panels—an oval, egg-shaped head with two dark eyes and large, protruding ears. Was this hideous sight me? I lifted my arms to touch my head, but revolted by the reflected image, I dropped my hands, denying for a moment the shock, the nightmare that was me.

We were pushed and shoved until we found ourselves in a large tiled area. Metal shower heads sprouted out of the ceiling. We stared at them in speechless terror. We had heard it whispered that these innocent-looking shower heads released a deadly gas that had already sent thousands to their deaths. We waited agonizing seconds until finally a thin stream of cold water fell on our shaven heads, ran over our stooped shoulders, and ended in a puddle around our feet. There were no towels. Dripping and frightened, we were herded into yet another barracks.

The stout SS woman followed close behind and shrieked at one of the other guards, "What an ugly bunch! Too bad the gas chambers are overworked today. But we'll get them another day. There's plenty of time—if they're still around!" Their laughter filled us with foreboding.

The second barracks building was large and filled with stacks of neatly folded garments. Behind each pile of clothing stood a Kapo. We were thrown a rag that remotely resembled a dress, but we were given neither underwear nor shoes, except for one woman who, without rhyme or reason, was thrown a pair of wooden clogs; I later found out that her name was Alice. Once dressed, we looked Kafkaesque, insane creatures ready for a costume party: skin and bones, ragged and shapeless, grotesque and shorn. I was close to hysterics. If only I could hide my head. Would my hair ever grow back? Would there be time?

Outside, the sun was bright and strong in spite of the early morning hour. Again we lined up in rows of five. Elli and I marched side by side down the camp avenue, our bare feet on the hot, sandy ground. Barbed wire and watchtowers surrounded us; machine guns targeted our group. Now other sounds reached us. Music. Music? Beethoven? Elli and I stared at each other and then at the musicians assembled on a wooden platform in the middle of the compound. Prisoners like us, their bare heads glistened in the sunlight. Their blue-and-gray-striped uniforms swayed rhythmically in time with the conductor's baton. The conductor was a German in an impeccable SS uniform. Unbelievable!

Our disbelief was quickly overtaken by a new wave of fear. We were marching past wooden barracks very much like the ones we had just left—except these sprouted tall chimneys that spit forth billowing clouds of acrid, black smoke. Frantic whispers ran from row to row: "Crematorium ... crematorium ..."

"What is it?" I half-mumbled.

"They're for burning bodies," someone answered. "They're burning bodies now."

A surge of horror shook my body. "Burning bodies?" I repeated the words, trying to make sense of them, but they reverberated, empty and meaningless, in my head. I was totally devoid of feelings.

Mechanically, I continued marching until a woman's harsh voice commanded, "Achtung! Halt! These barracks will be your shelter for the time being. I am the Kapo here. My name is Maja, and I want to warn you now to obey all orders or you'll be beaten or shot."

I thought she might be Jewish. She was tall, with black, short-cropped hair, high cheekbones, and deep brown eyes. She certainly was not suffering from hunger; not even the striped prison uniform could hide her curves. A barely audible voice inquired about food. Maja responded by laughing in short, shrill bursts. On command, we were pushed inside the wooden building, Maja using her stick on our backs to hurry us along. The building was divided down the center by a wide walkway. On each side were small cubicles, about five feet by five feet, separated by a narrow wooden strip on the floor.

"Five women to each cubicle," Maja shouted.

There was barely enough room for five women to sit at the same time, much less lie down. Jammed together, we sat in silence until Elli came up with an idea. "I have a solution. We might be able to sort of lie down during the night."

She sat down against the wall, her legs spread apart. She motioned for the next person to sit between her legs, and we continued the chain until all five of us sat in this manner. To stretch out, we had to rest our shaven heads on the stomach of the person behind us. Turning or moving was impossible. We sat listlessly. No one felt like talking; our thoughts were turned inward, and we were afraid to voice our fears. When evening finally came, a single bulb was lighted and threw an eerie glow on the shifting chain of women.

Suddenly, Maja's raspy voice shouted, "Line up for the latrines!"

We marched outside and across the adjacent open lot to another barracks building marked "Latrine." But there were no toilets, just holes in the ground, and no paper. The stench was unbearable. The connecting washroom consisted of a large metal trough with several spigots but no soap or towels. The faucets, when opened, dripped brown water. We each took our turn.

Back in the barracks, we were again confronted by Maja. "Tomorrow at dawn, you'll line up outside for Appell [roll call]. Straight rows of five, in alphabetical order."

Maja's latest bit of information gave us cause for alarm. This new ruling might mean a permanent separation for Elli and me, since her last name started with an S, mine with an L. We wanted to be able to stay together and face whatever fate might await us. I was worried and close to tears.

"We'll stand with the S group," I suggested. "They have no records of our names, and we no longer have papers. If they should ask, I'll tell them that I was married to your brother in the ghetto. They can't prove anything now."

Elli did not look convinced. "But what if they find out somehow?" Finally, she nodded a reluctant agreement. I was relieved, and the other three in our group followed my suggestion, each thinking of a name that started with an S.

It was dark and chilly inside the barracks, and we longed for food. Almost an entire day had passed since our arrival in Auschwitz, and it had been even longer since we had had anything to eat or drink. Our stomachs rumbled painfully in protest. Finally, several women prisoners in striped uniforms brought three large metal milk cans full of soup. They carried ladles but no bowls or plates. How were we to eat soup without a bowl or plate? Nevertheless, the starving women lined up and began slurping their soup out of dirty, dripping palms.

After a few puzzled moments, Elli looked at Alice. "Your shoes," she said. "We can use your shoes! Quick, take them off!" Alice complied. Elli took one shoe and started toward the soup line; Alice followed with the second shoe. Our eyes were fixed on them as they stood in line, waiting to have the wooden shoes filled with food. I hoped that there would be enough soup for the five of us. They returned with a steaming mess of liquid and turnips. Hungrily they put their mouths to the wooden clogs, devouring the contents like animals, and then passed the shoes to us. We got in line and waited impatiently for our turn. For the moment, hunger blanked out the image of pigs eating out of dirty, wooden troughs, but after we had finished, we looked at each other, silently revolted by our degradation.

The first night was cramped and painful on the hard floor. Using Elli's idea, we tried to sleep with our heads on the belly of the person behind us. At least the closeness kept us warm. There was nothing left of our personal belongings or of our former selves. I saw myself as an animal and realized that I would probably not leave Auschwitz alive.

Maja's shouts awakened us before dawn. She continued

screaming until we stood in straight lines of five, counting off one by one, until the total number of our group matched her log. We stood at attention, shivering in the early dawn, and wondered if anyone would check our names. No one did. We were forced to stand for almost five hours. As noon approached, the hot sun burned our shaven scalps and the rims of our ears. The salt from our perspiration added its own painful sting. Those who fainted from the heat or dropped from exhaustion were dragged away, never to be seen again. We began to look at the electrified barbed wire surrounding us as one way to end our misery. Some courageous women ran to the charged wires, touched them, and, after a short convulsion, dropped to the ground dead. Although many of us struggled to maintain hope, we hardly knew why or for what.

One evening, shortly after our arrival, Maja announced that after Appell, Dr. Mengele would inspect the prisoners. "The procedure is simple," she said. "You take off your dress, carry it in the left hand, and walk naked past the SS inspection team. Be fast and don't talk. They'll decide."

"Decide what?" I whispered to Elli.

"I've heard rumors that Mengele selects some for work, some for hospital experiments, and some for the gas chambers," Elli whispered in response. Once again, the SS would determine life and death.

That night, I tried to sleep, but I was preoccupied with thoughts of the inspection. My body was drained of energy, but images of the crematorium with its black smoke ravaged my mind. I wondered what it was like inside.

Morning broke, gray and dismal, and again we lined up, Elli and I still together. We stood and waited, our scantily clad bodies shivering. Three SS officers suddenly marched into the center of the Appellplatz.

"Attention!" Maja commanded.

"The one with the baton is Mengele," someone whispered. "He is God here. He'll sentence us—to work, to the gas chambers, or the hospital."

Elli looked at me, her eyes wide, her lips quivering. My heart, racing with fear, was about to explode. I suddenly realized that the minutes were numbered for many of us; yet my mind denied death as a possibility for me. Perhaps I would be sent to the hospital? But for what? It was beyond my understanding.

Maja now faced us. "Achtung! Remove dresses! Carry them in your left hand. First row, march—fast. Don't dally!"

Those in front of us almost ran past the three SS officers, while Mengele appraised them like cattle, motioning—right, left, right, left. His face was expressionless, almost casual.

"Next row!"

Elli nudged me, whispering, "Walk fast, don't look at anyone."

Shamefully I began running naked across the open field, forcing myself not to think. Dress in hand, I stumbled past the Germans, who stood no more than two or three feet away. I raced on, avoiding their stares, but out of the corner of my eye I saw the swinging baton in Mengele's hand motion me to the right. Was right better than left? Elli followed close behind and was also signaled to the right. Realizing that we were still together, we breathed a sigh of relief. At least half of the group had been directed to the left and were already being led away. We soon lost sight of them.

Next, we were ordered to follow Kapo Maja to another barracks. Were these the gas chambers?

Once inside, we saw a long table with clothing and Kapos standing behind it. As we passed by the table, the Kapos threw each of us a pair of old shoes, either too large or too small, and a ragged garment that vaguely resembled a coat. It was only then that I realized that small, skinny Alice was no longer with us.

Dressed in our new finery, we were marched past barbed wire to another section of the camp. In front of us on railroad tracks stood a line of cattle cars, their sliding doors wide open like gaping black holes.

"Schnell, hurry, and get into the cars!" Maja commanded.

It appeared that we were being sent on to another place. While we jostled each other to get into the crammed trains, Maja stood outside laughing hysterically. Once we were crowded into the boxcars, the doors were slammed shut and locked from the outside. With a sudden jolt, the train began to move.

We did not know where we were going or why; still, no one spoke. Mengele's inspections, anxiety, and the lack of food and water had taken their toll. Inside the cattle car, it was so stifling we could hardly breathe, much less speak. On the second day, we removed all of our clothing. When the train stopped on the third day, the bolts were thrust back and the doors thrown open. Outside, SS guards were waiting with guns.

"Raus, schnell! This is the work camp at Dessauer Ufer—Hamburg, Germany."

The Scarf ~

1944

> *"Left, right,*
> *Left, right"—*
> *An army of women,*
> *The column marched,*
> *Skeletons*
> *With empty stomachs,*
> *Ragged and shorn.*
> *"Left, right,*
> *Left, right,*
> *Don't straggle,*
> *Left, right,*
> *Left, right"—*
> *"Arbeit macht frei!"*
> *"Left, right,*
> *Left, right"—*
> *Those who dropped—*
> *Were shot.*

I was one of five hundred women who had passed Mengele's dreaded inspection; for the time being, we were considered able to work. Our reward was transportation in cattle cars from Auschwitz to Arbeitslager Dessauer Ufer for forced manual labor.

Our work was hard, clearing bomb damage in and around the city of Hamburg. We worked in shipyards removing heavy steel girders that were twisted and torn and shards of glass, remainders of huge windowpanes. Only with tremendous effort were we able to move and lift the wreckage. The rubble, it struck me, resembled my own life; nothing remained of the past but irreparably damaged bits and pieces and fragmented memories.

It was now November 1944, more than three years since my family's deportation to Lodz. The fall weather on the outskirts of Hamburg, Germany, was cool and damp with an almost continuous drizzle. A fine curtain of rain settled on our shaven heads and skimpily clad shoulders. By the end of each day we were soaked, our flimsy clothing drenched. Most of us coughed and were sick but were forced to work anyway. It was work or die.

We were assigned to a construction site that was wide open and unprotected from the elements. We marched—or tried to march—on thin legs, dragging wet oversized shoes or clogs on our frozen feet, trying desperately to keep the pace set by the braided whips of our SS guards.

Ahead of me, next to me, and behind me were rows of ugly shaven globes protruding from shabby clothing, given less for warmth than for identification. Each dress had a wide stripe of yellow cloth sewn into the front, the fabric underneath having been cut away. Every coat was splashed from seam to seam across the hips with a broad, yellow, oil-painted stripe. Stitched into each thin, scratchy coat on the left side above the breast was an oblong, yellow patch, stamped with a black Star of David. In the center of the star was the word *Jude*.

I still wished for something to cover my bald head, but not because of the cold wind or driving rain. It was, of all things, vanity. I thought of my once long, shiny brown hair and wondered if vanity was still possible. Who cared? What did anything really matter? But for some strange reason, it still mattered to me—even beyond the pain of my frostbitten toes, icy hands, and rain-drenched body.

Our guards were bundled in heavy green overcoats, plastic rain ponchos to match, hats with earmuffs, and long black leather gloves. The Obersturmbannführer in charge of our work group was about fifty years old. He was proud of his well-fitting uniform, of the Iron Cross around his neck, of his holstered revolver and the braided leather whip he nervously twisted in his right hand. His smile was vicious and was made even uglier by a missing front tooth. "Look at you women," he would yell angrily, "emaciated skeletons, not a beauty among you, dressed in rags, coughing most of the day!"

His right leg was stiff and a bit shorter than the left; it was probably wooden. We gave him the German nickname "Der zahnlose Lahme" (the toothless lame one). He often muttered to himself, just loud enough for us to hear, "What kind of a job is this for a man who has fought at the front? Guarding a group of crazy women...I earned the Iron Cross —paid for it with a leg." His mad chuckle would dissolve into a sick laugh, then he would continue, "We hid in trenches. They took their time, but they came in the end, at night, with flares and tanks. They were well equipped, well fed—we were no match for them. They left only blood, open bellies, eyes torn from their sockets, and splintered limbs— mine one of them!"

When his high-pitched voice reached a certain fury and violence, we knew he would find a target. "Bitches, I'll show you what the lame one can do!" He would yank his revolver from its holster and, grabbing the barrel in his right hand, vent his frustration and venom by hitting the women closest to him. One, two, three—we lost count as the women fell, their blood spattering on the ground. "Bitches, Jews, filthy Jews, it's all your fault."

His fury spent, he would stick the revolver into its holster, turn, and limp away, a lopsided figure in an SS uniform. Not until later, much later, would we dare to help the victims. However, without bandages or water to clean their wounds, we could give only the comfort of word and touch.

We were in our second week of hard labor when, among the rubbish I was moving and sorting into neat piles, I spotted a long, dirty piece of cloth in splashy shades of rust red and olive green. For several seconds, I stood mesmerized by the threadbare cloth. I was obsessed with longing for it but tried to bring myself to reason. We had been warned with threats of beatings or death not to take anything. Was my vanity really worth the risk? For what? I had no answers, but I already knew that I would take it and risk whatever punishment followed.

Carefully, I looked to make sure that I was not being observed. Then, I began gently pushing the scarf along with the rubble. Waiting for the right moment, I took my time, my heart beating faster and faster. I inched the rubble along, never losing sight of the priceless rag. Then, in one unobserved second, I bent down, took the scarf with my right hand, and slipped it between my thighs. A hot surge of triumphant joy swept through my shivering body. The rag, the scarf, was mine.

"Lunch break, line up, hurry!" Our meager lunch consisted of blood sausage and a small piece of bread. I could hardly swallow the red, spotted mess of meat; the disgusting taste almost made me retch. Besides, I knew that once I had eaten a little food, the hunger pains would only increase. But beyond all that, the will to survive and the immediate hunger made me eat anything, even potato peels or leaves.

The ten-minute break was over. "Back to work, hurry! Lazy, stinking Jews, wasting time!" the Obersturmbann-führer shouted as he snapped his whip. He had returned to observe our group.

We resumed the same, hard, tedious work. The Ober-sturmbannführer was calm now, his morning's anger spent. My head was bent, and I concentrated on my work. I did not dare look up. But I could see his shiny black boots as they approached my pile of neatly stacked bricks. I shuddered.

"You there! I need you to translate for me. Follow me to the back of the chimney." Even before he had spit out the last word, I could hear the leather whip wheeze through the air and winced in anticipation of its stinging pain. As it struck my shoulder, I looked up for the first time.

"Yes, you, don't stare like an idiot, hurry!"

"Jawohl, Herr Obersturmbannführer." I scurried and scrambled after him, trying to walk as fast as I could. I stumbled often over the rubble, my feet unable to stay inside the huge shoes. I worried about the scarf—had the German seen me take it?

As we approached the red brick chimney, all that remained of a large industrial building, I wondered who was working here who might be in need of translated orders. I noticed that the German's leather whip was now stuck into the top of his right boot, his gloves in the left. He passed the chimney and stepped quickly behind it. I followed.

At the far side, he abruptly came to a halt and turned,

stopping me in my tracks. As he spun around, his right arm swung around my neck and his large, cold hand covered my mouth. My God, the scarf—the penalty for stealing! I trembled.

His left hand moved swiftly down my body. I no longer doubted that he knew my secret. My absurd vanity would be my death. My head was still in his viselike grip as his hand came to a stop between my legs. He fingered the scarf. I stopped breathing, convinced that my life was over. Suddenly, he shouted into my ear, "You filthy, useless bitch! Pfui! Menstruating!" He pushed me away in disgust.

In a blank frenzy, I managed to run back to my work detail, the scarf still in its place. I couldn't speak. I looked around. No one had noticed my absence; no one cared. Now the shock of what had happened washed over me, leaving me weak and faint.

That night in the barracks, I gently washed my priceless rag in cold, soapless water. In the morning, I tied the still-damp scarf around my shaven head.

The Infirmary ∿

1944

My new treasure temporarily satisfied my vanity. My friends eyed the rag with envy; the guards seemed not to notice. Although the scarf covered my humiliation and provided me with some small sense of dignity, it did nothing to satisfy my ever-present hunger.

Bread remained in short supply, and the daily slice was devoured in seconds. Even after years of meager rations, our empty, rumbling stomachs refused to adjust to the lack of food and protested loudly and angrily. We dreamed of bread, fantasized about bread, and imagined a never-depleted, warm loaf that we would eat slice by slice, savoring and chewing each morsel until all desire for another piece had vanished. Hunger created the dream; hunger woke us to reality.

I continued to work in shipyards and on building sites, sorting rubble, stone, and glass from the previous months' bombings. My hands were bruised, cut, and painfully in-flamed from handling the dirty, rough remnants of what had been buildings, windows, and doors, fragments of a peaceful existence that I had almost forgotten. One day I cut the palm of my right hand while lifting a jagged piece of glass. During the days that followed, the deep gash became swollen and red. A narrow pink stripe started at the palm, traveled up the side of my arm, and came to a stop just above the elbow. My friend Sabina, who was working next to me, saw my contorted face and the hand that hung limp at my side.

"What is it?" she asked.

"Look at my hand and my arm!"

She gasped. "This is serious, you have to report it, something has to be done immediately!"

"Report? To them . . . the SS?"

"Yes, you no longer have a choice."

I thought about Mrs. Korn and the previous evening's public beating. Mrs. Korn always walked next to her sixteen-year-old daughter but never quite managed to keep in step with the rest of the group. She was a large-boned woman, whose once-bleached hair was shorn; she appeared old and haggard but was probably only in her midforties. She looked grotesque, with her huge head resting on a thin toothpick of a neck. Long, apelike arms dangled at her sides, and her short, thin legs ended in enormous flat feet. She had spent the ghetto years as the pampered and privileged wife of the Jewish ghetto police chief; she had received ample food in those days, and the hardships of others in the ghetto had left her personally untouched. Here, as just another worker, she had been unable to adjust to conditions at the camp.

Yesterday, returning from the work site, she had trailed off to the side of the road and straggled behind, unable to walk faster. The Hauptsturmführer, a short, impatient man with cruel, squinty eyes, watched us return from work to the old warehouses at Dessauer Ufer, where we slept on the bare wood floors. His eyes fixed on Mrs. Korn, and the sight of her was more than he could bear. Once inside the building, he flew into a rage and foamed like a mad dog. He called her out of the line, made her kneel in the middle of the floor, and ordered us to form a circle around her. We had stood, rows of silent, terrified witnesses as he beat her with a heavy leather strap.

She screamed. He counted. His fury seemed boundless. Finally, she collapsed. We stared at the barely breathing heap of flesh on the blood-spattered boards, but we were not permitted to help her.

Tomorrow it could be me—beaten or shot. Sabina nudged me, interrupting my thoughts. "Go now," she whispered.

I approached the Obersturmführer guarding our work group. "Prisoner Landau asks for permission to speak," I said in German. Silently, he looked at me in disgust, but I took this as a sign that I could continue. "My hand—it is infected. I would like to have it cleaned so I can work better . . ." My voice trailed off. Fearfully, I stretched out my hand so that he could see.

"You are a damned nuisance," he said, but he didn't look at my hand. His face was without expression, without pity. "I will report this to the commandant later."

"Jawohl," I managed to say and hurried away.

The evening was quiet. My hand was throbbing and painful, and I spent a sleepless night worrying. Dawn finally came, another gray, rainy day, and we hurriedly dressed and lined up in groups of five for Appell. We counted off as usual. Then suddenly I heard my name: "Prisoner Landau, step forward."

I took one small, very tentative step forward.

"Follow the SS guard to the truck!" a voice barked.

I scrambled down the stairs of the warehouse to the entrance, and there stood a truck. The motor of the long flatbed was coughing and spitting, and the engine rattled loudly. "Climb into the truck!" someone yelled. I pulled myself up and slid backward against the cab. A pair of hands grabbed me from behind and tied my left arm to the siderails with thick, rough rope. I was afraid to turn around, but I heard him—or someone—jump off the truck, open the door of the cab, and slam it shut. The engine roared as the truck began to move. Crouched in the back, I shivered as the rain began to soak through my clothes. The folded tarp in the opposite corner would have offered protection, but I knew it was not meant for me. Next to me was a huge boiler attached to the cab with steel bands. The boiler was filled to the top with small pieces of wood. Amazing! Using wood instead of gasoline, the Germans still managed to keep their vehicles moving!

Alone with my fear and the shooting pain in my arm, I wondered where they were taking me. Would I return? Would they kill me? For what seemed like hours, the truck drove through unfamiliar areas, down country roads and narrow streets, until it slowed in front of a huge Auschwitz-like compound. The truck rumbled through the guarded gates. The camp was surrounded by barbed wire and watchtowers, and the sign read:

Konzentrationslager Neuengamme

I had heard that our camp was an Aussenlager (branch) of Neuengamme, but until this moment the words had been meaningless, and I had no idea why they had brought me here.

"Down from the truck!" yelled the same harsh voice.

"I can't move," I answered. "I'm tied to the rails."

Behind me, several hands pulled on the rope, untied me, and pushed me off the truck. I fell and hurriedly got up again. All around me, every ten feet, were uniformed SS guards. Their stern, unsmiling faces reminded me of Auschwitz. Their guns were shouldered, and they seemed to pay no attention to me, as if I did not exist. I stood near the gate and waited. Suddenly a boot kicked my lower back, and I was propelled with a rifle butt through the door of a small barracks. Inside stood several male prisoners. Their striped prison uniforms were crumpled and dirty. They eyed me curiously, the only female in the room. SS guards stood near the door.

"No talking, no touching, absolute quiet," a faceless voice in back of us yelled.

Not daring to turn around, I stared straight ahead through a small window, heavily barred from the outside. I saw a huge Appellplatz, deserted except for two guards walking on either side of a prisoner. He was an elderly, stooped man in striped prison garb, who seemed small and frail. He walked slowly. I wondered who he was and whether he was enjoying a privilege or being punished. A voice whispered, "Prime Minister Léon Blum."

The name sounded familiar, but I couldn't place it. Judging from the name, I knew he was a Jew, but from where? My eyes continued to follow his slow, dragging steps.

My thoughts were interrupted by a loud voice: "Prisoner

Landau, outside, hurry! Don't stand there like an idiot. Load the eight cardboard boxes into the truck. Be fast, and cover them with the tarp."

When I tried to lift the boxes, my right hand throbbed so painfully I almost screamed, but I pushed and tugged and finally managed to get them into the truck. Resentfully, I covered the boxes with the tarp, envious of their protection from the rain.

Again, my left hand was tied to the rails. Two SS men sat in the cab laughing and smoking, warm and comfortable. Silently, I cursed them. The motor revved and the truck lunged forward. Now we passed through an area that was desolate and deserted, the buildings partially bombed out, burned shells with blackened walls and gaping windows without glass. The few civilians we passed paid no attention to the truck, even though the SS man drove recklessly and at high speed. We turned a corner, narrowly missing a huge, empty crater in the center of the street. The sign on the corner read, "Spaldingstrasse."

The truck came to an abrupt stop in front of a huge warehouselike building, the walls blackened by fire and soot. The cab opened and the two SS guards got out, climbed into the flatbed, and untied my hand. "Out, down, hurry," they growled. Awkwardly, I scrambled down from the truck and walked several paces behind the guards as they saluted their counterparts at the front entrance: "Heil Hitler!" with right arms raised high.

Once inside the dark corridors, I noticed several men wearing blue-and-gray-striped prison uniforms with matching caps. We exchanged curious glances. A strange place...

Was this an Arbeitslager like ours? I was not sure. I entered a room through a door marked "Infirmary."

"Stand here and don't dare move," shouted my escort. "You'll be called!"

The room was large and empty except for two windows at the far end, which were covered with plywood. Against the wall stood an oblong table; two naked light bulbs hung from long, dirty cords attached to the wood-raftered ceiling. The walls were concrete, a reddish brown color, and the wooden floors were worn but clean. Next to the table, with their backs turned, stood an SS officer and several prisoners. A few inches from my feet, a thin, tired-looking young man in striped prison rags moved back and forth on his knees, washing the floor with an incredibly filthy, torn rag. The skin of his face was drawn, wrinkled, and jaundiced. We cautiously smiled at each other. He whispered in a language I did not understand. I whispered back in German, "Lodz ghetto."

I wasn't sure if he understood, but he kept smiling.

"Deutschland kaput, gut, sehr gut!" he said, meaning that the war was almost over. But I had heard this refrain for the last three years, and the war still continued. I stopped smiling; our misery seemed endless. But what if he was right? Someone had to be right, finally? After all, the war had to end sometime.

The SS guard moved toward us, his voice screeching, "Scrub the floor, you idiot, don't dally! Get clean water, you pig!"

The young man jumped to his feet, stood at attention with cap in hand, and grabbed the bucket. The rag was still on the

floor as he walked away. For some reason, I desperately
wanted him to come back. Several minutes passed before he
reappeared with a bucket of clean water and resumed his
scrubbing, gently rocking back and forth on his knees. His
right hand disappeared under his jacket, and he removed a
small ball of dirty, crumpled paper and put it gently next to
my feet. He pointed to the package, took his bucket, and
moved on. The guard was talking to someone else. I waited
to make sure that I would not be seen, then quickly picked
up the package. As I slipped it into my left pocket, I could
feel a dry crust of crumbling bread through the paper. I
glanced over at the young man; I had nothing but a smile to
give him in return for his loving gift.

My thoughts were suddenly interrupted: "Next, Prisoner
Landau!" I walked forward, taking large, quick steps across
the room until I reached the table.

"Was ist denn los mit Dir?" the voice of the Unterscharführer in front of me grumbled. He was a well-fed middle-
aged man in a clean uniform. His pants were tucked into
shiny, black boots. He did not wear a white coat, and the
name tag on his chest read: "Unterscharführer—Sanitäter."

A medical corpsman? Damn him, I thought, not even a
real doctor.

"Well, answer my question!" He was impatient now.

I stretched out my right hand, palm up, but said nothing.

He looked at the palm. "Where did you get that? And
when did it happen?"

"Several days ago, at the work site of Blom and Foss Shipyards."

"Hmmm . . . you speak correct German—how come?"

"I went to high school in Hamburg until 1941, when I graduated from the Oberrealschule (gymnasium)."

The SS man frowned. "So you say, but it better not be a lie! Do you understand Plattdeutsch?" Plattdeutsch was a local Hamburg dialect.

"Jawohl, Herr Doktor."

"What do you answer to Hummel-Hummel?"

Before I had time to think, the words slipped out of my mouth, "Mors, Mors!" meaning "Kiss my ass."

The German's jowls shook with merriment, and his stubby torso rocked back and forth. "Ha, you passed the test. Only a person familiar with Hamburg folklore would know the legend of the old water carrier the kids nicknamed Hummel-Hummel, and his angry reply." He repeated, "Mors, Mors," and laughed.

The joke finished, he became serious and called two prisoners, men with gray, sallow skin and sunken eyes, to help me sit on the table. One man held me, the second pulled my hand forward and gripped it tightly. The corpsman, knife in hand, looked at me. "I don't want to hear you scream when I lance the infection."

I nodded, terrified in anticipation of the pain. He wore thin rubber gloves through which I could see his short, fat fingers and strong, long nails, white and clean. He suspended the knife over my hand for a few moments, then pierced the wound. I felt hot pain followed by the taste of blood in my mouth. Then more pain as hands squeezed the palm and touched the infected area. I became weak and leaned against the prisoner who held me. I could feel his bony arms and his sunken chest through the rough fabric of his uniform. I could not see his face, but his foul-smelling breath told me it was near mine. I could barely breathe, but my jaws remained clenched. Not a sound was to escape. I can do it . . . I must do it, I thought. Please, don't let me faint, I begged as the darkness overcame me.

When I opened my eyes, the doctor's face was close to mine. "You fainted," he said, "but at least you didn't scream!"

It was almost a compliment. My palm burned and stung as he doused it with liquid. The doctor bandaged the hand. The white, fresh gauze turned red almost immediately. More layers, and still the blood soaked through.

"Finished, go, and don't dare to come back!" he barked.

"Jawohl, Herr Doktor. Thank you, Herr Doktor."

He was gruff but at least not cruel and vindictive. It could have been worse. I thought again about Mrs. Korn.

As I slid down from the table with the help of the prisoner with the foul breath, I could feel his hand in my left pocket. The bread—he was trying to steal my bread! But before I could react, he had stuffed another package into the already bulging pocket. He still stood in back of me, and I could not see his face. I walked to the door, where the two SS men who had brought me were waiting. For one brief moment, I glanced back at the prisoners and whispered a silent thank you and good-bye.

I was returned to my little corner of the truck, my left arm again tied to the rails. The bouncing of the speeding truck over rough, uneven pavement made me sick. My head ached and my hand throbbed in excruciating pain. Slowly, I removed the two small packages from my pocket. The first contained a roll of clean white gauze to bandage my hand.

The second contained a dry piece of bread. I chewed hungrily on the half-eaten crust. I felt weak but strangely happy. I could still see the drawn, yellow faces of the men in the infirmary, their bony, dirty fingers reaching out and holding me.

Icy rain drops mingled with my hot tears.

Liberation ~

1945

At the gravesite
Liberators
In huge, green
Bulldozers
Covered with mud,
Churn the damp, warm earth
Until a black gaping pit
Embraces
The stench of greenish bodies—of nameless
Men, women, and children
Killed by hate.

The chaplain recites his prayer.
His words speak gently, painfully,
Of the past and present:
"Our dead—never to be forgotten."
Their desperate, pleading voices
Ring in my ears.
The sky spins above me,
Spins like a balloon,
And the ground under my feet
Heaves and crumbles
Into nothingness.

I open my eyes
To the touch of gentle, soft hands,
A caring face,
In a sun-drenched blue-walled room.
Outside:
Bulldozers still

Whine and work,
Their revving, screaming engines
Unearthing
Years of pent-up
Pain: I weep for those
In the gaping, black pit—
Their deaths
My eternal unrest.

Soon after my visit to the infirmary, our entire group of five hundred women was transferred from Dessauer Ufer to Arbeitslager Sasel. It was a small, newly erected camp, with barbed wire, watchtowers, and barely enough barracks space to house us. We were assigned to work in the surrounding areas, building "Plattenhäuser"—new homes constructed of large, heavy concrete sheets—for Germans who had been bombed out of their residences. Once again we were subjected to extreme physical labor and exposed to the winter's rain, snow, and sleet.

Somehow word got around that Sofie, a young attorney from Lodz, and I spoke fluent German, and we were ordered to work in the "Schreibstube" (office). Although the work allowed us protection from the outdoors, it did not protect us from the savage beatings and abuse of the SS. Our work consisted of keeping handwritten records of all incoming rations used for SS personnel and prisoners, as well as updating daily the roster of names and addresses of the entire SS staff. Writing was not easy. My hand still had not healed.

After four months at Arbeitslager Sasel, in March of

1945, we were suddenly ordered into trucks. Elli and I sat cramped together, wondering what would happen next. It was several hours before we approached what looked like another concentration camp. There was the same iron gate at the entrance, the same barbed wire all around, the same rows upon rows of barracks in the distance.

As we were ordered off the trucks and started marching into the camp, we couldn't help noticing to the right and left of our column several large mountains of shoes. There were large shoes, small shoes, old shoes, new shoes—nothing but shoes. I could only guess where the owners of these shoes might be.

The usual grapevine passed the news from row to row in barely audible whispers: "Bergen-Belsen." Once again we were herded and pushed into one barracks building, far too small to hold almost five hundred women.

Our first day there was quiet except for the occasional shrieks and moans of a young woman lying on the floor not far from us.

Elli and I walked over and stood beside her. We did not know what to do to help her. We finally put her rolled-up coat under her head and spoke to her, but she could only cry out in pain. As the night faded into morning, her piercing shrieks became more frequent and intense. Then suddenly, she was quiet. To our horror, we found that she had given birth to a stillborn infant weighing hardly more than two pounds.

"I didn't even know I was pregnant," the woman sobbed. Tears ran down her bony, sunken cheeks. "It has been eight months . . . the separation from my husband . . . Auschwitz!"

We held her hands and hoped that she would fall asleep.

Someone picked up the baby, wrapped it in a rag, and took it away. I wondered what they would do with it.

In the early morning hours, I had to go to the latrine. On the way, I encountered some women dragging their tired, emaciated bodies with each step. They looked at me, the seemingly able-bodied newcomer, with accusing eyes; they knew that compared to the other camps, this was one of the worst.

"Are you looking for the latrines? We've been here for more than six months; we'll show you the way."

The inside of the building was incredibly filthy. The latrine was merely a hole in the ground, and the washroom faucets dripped only a few drops of water at a time. The smell was almost unbearable. Outside, the women pointed to a huge open pit filled with decaying, dead bodies—the infants' burial ground.

"Do the Germans send in food?" I asked.

"Lately there has been practically no food at all. They leave a large can of thin soup at the gate, and the Kapos give us barely half a bowl a day. And there is no work, only typhus all around us. Not a barracks has been spared. The Germans no longer enter the camp because they are afraid of the typhus."

After the shock of that first day, I began to lose track of time. Days and nights ran into each other. I was growing weaker and more listless; I had lost all interest in living. It was obvious that we could not survive much longer. Elli and I sat on the floor for hours on end, quiet and resigned. Nothing mattered anymore—we had ceased to feel human, even to ourselves. Inside and out, the stench of decay engulfed us; we were constantly surrounded by the smell, the taste, the sounds of disease, death, and despair.

"How many days have passed, Elli? How long have we been here?"

"I don't know; it seems like an eternity. I only know that we will last only a few days longer."

I nodded.

It was an unusually quiet morning. The sky was overcast The guard towers were manned, and as usual, the SS kept their machine guns aimed at us. But something was different ...odd. Although the SS wore their usual uniforms, they had added white armbands. We wondered what it might mean.

At noon Elli and I stood outside the barracks, the sun straight overhead. Suddenly, the ground trembled beneath our feet, and a rumbling noise filled the air. Cautiously, we ventured toward the middle of the compound, then closer to the barbed wire that separated us from the main camp road. There, we saw tanks—huge, crawling monsters beginning to line the street from end to end. The men on top of the tanks wore khaki uniforms. We watched, stunned and bewildered. A woman's shrill, hysterical cry pierced the air as she pointed to the soldiers, "Look, they're British ... They've come, the war must be over! We are free!"

We watched with both fear and disbelief. Could it be true? We stood motionless until the soldiers jumped off the tanks and walked toward the camp gate. Some of us began to cry, others cheered and laughed as several uniformed British officers entered the camp. The Germans seemed suddenly to have disappeared. The women pressed against the fence and the gate, now guarded by the soldiers in khaki. We followed their every gesture, still not sure that these were our liberators.

Finally, one of them spoke to us in English. "We have liberated this camp. But we are not prepared for what we have found and seen with our own eyes. We'll try to rush in food, water, and medical supplies."

So it was true. We were liberated—finally! Tears, laughter, hugging, and uncontrollable senseless screams burst out of us. The British watched in silence, staring at us, their eyes reflecting horror and disbelief. When we calmed down, the same soldier asked if anyone understood English.

Along with several others, I raised my hand.

"Good, we can use you. We need you to translate for us." They watched us carefully. They looked at our torn, filthy clothing and our thin faces, stained with tears. We saw the troubled bewilderment in their eyes.

I was immediately assigned to three officers. The tall one introduced himself. "I'm Major Brinton. I'm from Scotland. You'll get used to my accent," he laughed. "I'd like to see the inside of several barracks, talk to people, and ask some questions. You'll translate for me."

With more energy than I thought I could muster, I led the way. We walked into the nearest barracks building. Most of the women there had been too weak to come out; some were on the verge of death. The major asked for names, nationalities, and how long they had been in the camps. Most inmates cried; some tried to kiss the hands of the officers. All of them begged for food. I looked at the British. There was horror in their faces. They were unable to comprehend what they saw. They stared at human beings who were barely human, reduced to skeletons with burning eyes and halting voices, bearing little resemblance to women. These still-breathing collections of bones all hoped to live. Their hollow eyes followed us.

The compound housing the men was even worse. I had never been there before. These men had been in Bergen-Belsen a long time; they no longer talked or smiled. On a corner bunk, we saw a skeleton of a man, so emaciated that his skull showed every bone. He stared at us through sunken, feverishly blank, burning eyes. He held a knife in one hand, and as we watched, he slashed away at the thigh of a nearby corpse and then hungrily devoured the flesh. Two of the three officers turned and ran; the third vomited where he stood.

One of the officers screamed, "For Christ's sake, let's get some help!"

I was paralyzed. I had seen and experienced much, but this man left me shaken. What had we become? The Germans had succeeded in reducing us to subhumans. Would we ever be normal again? It seemed impossible. Despite our liberation, I was totally without hope.

The British were quiet. They had seen more than they had bargained for. "Enough for today. Come to the camp gate tomorrow morning at 8:00," they said to me, "and we'll see where we can use you."

The major pressed a small packet of biscuits and several cigarettes into my hand.

"Thank you," I murmured.

"Don't mention it," he sadly replied.

It was late when I returned to our barracks. Elli and I sat on the floor and shared the biscuits and cigarettes. We were silent, still too numb to comprehend all that had happened. Sleep was impossible. My mind raced with plans for the future. I'd have to write to my family in Palestine, in England, and in the United States. They had not heard from any of us in more than four years. They did not know that Mother and Father had been murdered. And Karin—where was she now? I could only wonder and hope. Maybe I would hear from her . . . maybe she would come to Hamburg . . . maybe. . . . I thought about our separation during the selection in the Lodz ghetto. Where had they taken her? Had she been liberated, too?

Even though liberation seemed to promise a return to a normal life, it did not bring happiness. Instead, it revived feelings that had long been numbed by the daily struggle for both mental and physical survival—feelings of guilt, loneliness, and utter devastation. The reality of liberation was so different from what I had imagined. I had dreamed of a great party, with fanfare, music, dancing, and fireworks. There was, however, only renewed sorrow for the dead and little hope for the living. Liberation had come quietly, and it had brought with it the realization that thousands of us had not lived to see this moment. Many of us would not live even until the end of the week.

It was almost midnight when the British troops managed to bring drinking water into the camp. This was followed by a huge supply of two-pound tins filled with pieces of pork and lard. Most of the former inmates gulped down the contents of the entire can in minutes. I still chewed on my biscuits, afraid to touch the pork. Within less than an hour, those who had eaten the pork were vomiting and writhing with stomach cramps. Elli and I walked outside; the smell inside the barracks had become more unbearable than ever. I decided to beg the British for more biscuits or bread until our stomachs could get used to food again.

As dawn broke the next morning, the five of us chosen to translate already stood at the gate. Finally, as the sun appeared on the horizon, the major and several officers arrived. The major wanted to know how long we had been waiting. When we told him, "Since daybreak," he looked perplexed. We explained that we had no watches, that they had been taken by the Germans in Auschwitz.

"Come with me," said the major.

For the first time since my arrival at Bergen-Belsen, the camp gate was opened for us, and we walked through it. We had never before left the confines of the camp, and walking into the former SS area without a single German confronting us seemed unbelievable.

We followed the major to the German barracks and stopped in front of a green building marked "Supplies." Inside, on tables, benches, and the floor were hundreds of boxes, neatly sorted and filled with ladies' watches, men's watches, rings, bracelets, brooches, and strings of pearls. Along the far wall were huge boxes filled to the brim with gold coins and foreign currency. We stared in stunned silence, reluctantly remembering Auschwitz and how these heirlooms had been torn from our arms, fingers, and necks. Piles of gold teeth, removed from the mouths of the dead, were hoarded here, destined for distribution or sale to Germans.

"I want each of you to choose a watch so you can be on time for work. Just make sure it still runs," the major said, rather matter-of-factly.

I stretched out my hand, only to pull it back. I wondered

about the owners. I could still see the faces of my fellow prisoners as they stood huddled, fearing the worst. Where were they now? Major Brinton's voice ended my ruminations: "Come on, make up your mind!"

I picked up a small, oblong silver watch, wound it, and saw the second hand move. Unbelievable! The back of the watch was slightly rusty, the leather strap black and worn. I put the watch around my wrist with a silent prayer that its owner was alive and that someday she would recognize the watch and claim it. She never did.

Several days after liberation, life at Bergen-Belsen started to take on a certain routine. My work as an interpreter kept me busy, and I momentarily forgot everything else. Food improved; there was hot stew now, dark bread, hot tea. No one went hungry. Still, hundreds died daily. For them, food and freedom had come too late.

Two weeks after I began working, I summoned enough courage to ask the major if I could shower or bathe. He looked at me, embarrassed. How could he understand? It had been almost four years.

"Of course. I'll make arrangements for you and the others," he said.

A young woman officer of the British Red Cross took the five of us to the showers in the former SS barracks. We were handed a small piece of soap and a towel. The showers worked! Hot water streamed over our cropped hair and thin bodies. It was heaven. I soaped and rinsed again and then again, hoping that perhaps the clean, hot water would put distance between the dark, bloody past and the present. But it didn't work. The past could not be forgotten, not then—perhaps not ever. I finally stepped outside, dried myself, and put on my ragged, dirty clothing. In time perhaps we would have new, clean clothes.

During the days that followed, huge bulldozers were brought into the camp. They dug deep craters. Then they shoveled the thousands of dead bodies that lay in a heap into the gaping pit. Those who could attended the services. I stood at the rim of the pit, listening to the army chaplain recite prayers in English and the Kaddish in Hebrew. Suddenly the earth heaved, my head spun, my arms flailed, and the world around me turned black.

Later, when I opened my eyes, I found myself in a light, airy room. A kind voice told me that I had fainted. Gentle hands were applying cool compresses to my head, and I burst into uncontrollable sobs. I could neither talk nor explain; no words could sound the depths of my pain and sorrow or articulate the agony of total loss.

Displaced Persons' Camp ～

1945

The war, for me, had ended on April 15, 1945, at Bergen-Belsen when I was liberated by the British Army. Liberation was still almost unbelievable. I had survived. No more beatings, hunger, or killings—yet the realities of liberation were not what I had expected. There was no euphoria or joy. But perhaps I was no longer capable of experiencing joy. I had daydreamed about life after the war. My dream was of a return to life the way it had been before the war: our sunny apartment, our close family, my friends, a navy silk dress with a full, sweeping skirt. Five years ago, I had been thinking of parties, dances, boys, going to art school. Instead of parties—mass murders. Instead of dances—Mengele's selections. Instead of my full sweeping skirt—a striped rag with a yellow star. Instead of art school—the art of death, dehumanization, and despair.

Until now I had not been conscious of the fact that the one short happy period of my life was gone, never to return. I was physically and emotionally scarred. My family and friends no longer existed. Everything and everyone important to my life were gone forever. Slowly I realized that I could not turn back to what had been but only toward something different, unknown, and uncertain. Even the future was blocked; I was still not free.

Like so many others, I became ill. We all suffered the aftereffects of malnutrition. Typhus and tuberculosis were the main problems. I vaguely recall drifting in and out of consciousness with a high fever but refusing to go to the hospital. My friend Sabina was dabbing my face, applying cool compresses to my hot forehead, and making me drink water My kidneys were not functioning well, and I was in constant, almost unbearable pain. Large boils began to appear on my neck and shoulders; they opened, drained, and healed, but new ones took their place. The British doctors had neither explanations nor medication; they thought the combination of dirt, unsanitary conditions, and a "deprived system" might be the cause.

"They'll disappear in six months. All you need is a regular diet," they told me. But when or where could one get it? The food that was cooked for us in army kitchens consisted of a piece of dark bread and a stew made with shredded, dried vegetables. There was no meat, fruit, or fresh vegetables, and no one had heard of vitamins.

Elli was so gravely ill that she was hospitalized. When I visited her, she looked pale and thin between the white sheets.

"Will I make it?" she whispered. "They tell me that I have diseased lungs and might need surgery. The war is over now, but I'm sicker than I ever was."

I held her hands and silently demanded, "Dear God, don't let her die now."

My visit a few days later threw me into a panic. Elli's bed

was empty. "Where have you taken her? What have you done with her?" I screamed at the nurses.

They tried to calm me down, explaining that they had sent her to a sanitorium in Switzerland where she would have surgery and the special care she needed. In a daze, I left the hospital feeling tired and sad, wondering if Elli and I would ever see each other again.

We were warehoused in large, red-brick barracks, the former German "Kasernen," which had been used as military housing for the German army. Six or seven women occupied one large room, slept in gray metal bunk beds, and shared a dormitory-type bathroom at the end of the hall. I longed for some privacy.

Although we were allowed free run of the entire camp, the British did not permit us to leave it. Sometimes these rules were ignored, and now and then someone would come back from a "trip" into occupied Germany with stories of the country's total defeat. They would often bring back little trinkets of china or jewelry, some of which had been bartered for, others stolen. "Why pay?" was the attitude. "Didn't the Germans take all our possessions, even the gold teeth from both the living and the dead?" Occasionally, there were incidents, altercations between displaced persons and German civilians, but the British tried to ignore them.

People were constantly inquiring about missing family members and friends. One woman, Hela, was looking for her father. "He was always tough, indestructible, a hard worker—I'm sure he must have survived."

But not a trace was to be found. He had been seen at Auschwitz. There the trail ended.

Sabina was luckier. She located her younger sister, Dzuta, through the Red Cross. She had been sent with a children's transport to Sweden. Sabina now concentrated on getting permission to enter Sweden.

Lola was looking for her mother. We heard that she had worked under horrible conditions in Mauthausen and had died there of hunger and exhaustion. Two women in her group had managed to survive, and the news of her death, passed from person to person, finally reached Lola.

I kept searching for any scrap of information about my sister and about Julie and Julius, the elderly couple who had befriended me in the ghetto. My inquiries always met with the same response: all of the children and old people deported from the ghetto in 1942 had been murdered by the Germans. Memories of Karin and of my unfulfilled promise to Mother haunted my nights and days. Karin's frightened, tearstained face kept reappearing. Coming to terms with the loss of Karin, of Mother and Father, was impossible. My desolation and despair over their deaths made me question my own right to survive. And I was alone with my guilt.

Almost daily, visitors from other camps arrived, straggling men and women who were traveling from camp to camp in search of their families. Some stayed, others made their way west, and some even returned to Poland. One morning an old friend, Chawa Levi, whom I had not seen for more than a year, stopped me on my way to work. We had worked together in the same office in the Lodz ghetto. She told me that she had walked and hitched rides from a camp in southern Germany in search of her younger sister, Dorka. She asked me if I had any information, but I could not help.

"I have talked to many of our former friends," she said,

"and I heard that Szaja is alive. He is supposed to be traveling back to Poland." Chawa's information took me by surprise. The mention of Szaja's name dredged up a mixture of feelings. I remembered our closeness, our walks through the ghetto streets, the love, the abandonment, his saving my life. It all seemed so very long ago, yet the feelings were alive, and the images remained vivid.

"Did he ask about me?" I queried.

"I have no idea," Chawa replied.

I still wanted him to care. I wondered if he would pass through Bergen-Belsen and look for me. I wished he would, but a little voice inside my head told me that he would not. As the months passed, I often thought about Szaja, but I never heard from him. I reasoned that he had probably returned to Lodz—a place I never wanted to see again. I resigned myself to memories.

Fortunately, my work forced me to confront each day and to live in the present. I hoped that this would keep me sane. I knew English and German, could manage Polish and French. I was working for Major Brinton, a burly man, dark-haired, dark-eyed, about six feet tall, with a bellowing voice. I worked as an interpreter and translator from 8:00 to 6:00, six days a week. Whenever he needed conversations and letters translated, he would call on me. He demanded fast, spontaneous translations and asked that they be only more or less accurate. Speaking English was a challenge, and my work and contact with the British helped me, at least for a few hours, to forget the past.

Displaced persons (DPs) were paid little, and the money we received, "Occupation marks," had been issued by the army for interim use until a stable currency could be established. The marks were worthless; one could buy very little with them. The real currency in occupied Germany was food, coffee, and cigarettes.

Most of my friends spent their days visiting, gossiping, and waiting for charitable organizations, such as the Hebrew Immigration Aid Society (HIAS) or the Joint Distribution Committee, to come and send them to a new home—that is, to any country willing to accept DPs. Few were willing. Furthermore, because we lived in a displaced persons' camp, it was almost impossible to obtain entry visas.

I had hoped to emigrate to Palestine or the United States where I had family and friends, but the war had left me without any documents—no passport, no birth certificate, no proof at all that I existed or that I was the person I said I was. Paris and London, the two cities with embassies from which one could obtain visas, were far away, and I lacked both the financial means and the proper documents to get there. I felt trapped in a bureaucratic nightmare. Nevertheless, my hopes for pursuing a normal life depended on getting out of Germany—Europe, if necessary—as quickly as possible. I had no intention of waiting.

I began to devise various schemes for leaving Germany. Since I had only limited power over my own destiny, my plots always involved contacting friends or family abroad, although this approach had its own obstacles. Postal service out of the country was not available to anyone except military personnel. I asked one of my British coworkers if I could use his name and APO number to write to family and friends in Palestine and the United States. He agreed. I immediately dashed off several letters, one to my uncle Herman, my father's brother in Palestine, others to friends in the U.S. and

Great Britain. I wanted them to know that I was alive and, more importantly, that my parents and my sister had been killed.

Finally, after a month's wait, my uncle's first letter reached me. I was overjoyed. As I mulled over his letter, I hit upon an idea. If I married a Palestinian citizen, I would be able to leave. In my reply, I asked my uncle if he would please, please, help get me out of Germany and into Palestine by marrying me.

A month passed before I received an answer. Uncle Herman wrote that he was old and ailing, no longer able to travel. However, he had contacted my cousin Fred, a cousin on my mother's side, who was stationed in Holland and serving in the Palestine brigade of the British army. He said that Fred had consented to marry me and that I could expect to hear from him soon. I would have preferred my uncle, but in desperation I was willing to marry anyone to get out. A divorce later would take care of such a marriage.

Returning from work one evening in July, I found Fred waiting for me. I recognized him by his striking resemblance to my mother and knew who he was before he even got up to embrace me. He was good-looking—my friends even thought handsome—in his late twenties, pleasant and well mannered. We took a long walk that evening; there was much I wanted to know about the family in Palestine, but mostly I wanted to know if he would indeed marry me.

"Of course I will," he answered immediately. "My parents think this is a very good idea." I was delighted with the news—but only for a moment. Casually, he continued, "Even though we are cousins, we can still have a wonderful life together."

I was stunned. Did he and his parents actually think that our marriage was to be permanent? For some reason, I had assumed that Fred knew that this arranged marriage was merely a device to get me out of Germany. Although his attitude promised to be yet another obstacle, I said nothing and decided to go ahead with my plan for a temporary marriage. Everything else could be worked out later; first, I simply had to get out. As we continued walking, I asked about his work as a civilian, what he did in his spare time, if he was interested in music or the theater, and whether he had any hobbies.

He said he worked as a carpenter, did not care for books, museums, or the theater. He spent his free time helping his parents around the house and garden and in their small food store. He did not have a car but rode a bike. He closed by telling me that I would enjoy their quiet little place in Palestine and that we would, of course, live with his parents.

He stayed only three days, but at the end of that time, I knew that if I did go through with the plan, I definitely would not stay married to him. He was kind but uninteresting. We had nothing in common other than the fact that his father and my mother were brother and sister. To think that the family had already decided on our marriage and had determined our future made me angry. I began to panic, but I tried to put all these feelings aside and concentrate on my main goal: getting out of Germany.

"I'll make the necessary arrangements with my commanding officer so we can marry as soon as possible. I'm sure the request will be granted." He looked happy, and I could tell that he fully intended to make this marriage a real and permanent arrangement. I was relieved when he left— and apprehensive about the future.

For the next six weeks, Fred's letters arrived regularly from Holland. The more he wrote, the more I knew that I could not possibly live with him. Still, he represented my best hope for getting out of Germany.

One morning, several weeks after Fred's visit, two British officers appeared in the office.

"Are you Cecilia Landau? We would like to talk to you."

"Of course," I replied quickly, pulling up some chairs. I knew that everyone who worked for the British was being investigated for security reasons, and I wanted to keep my job.

"Where were you born?" one of them continued.

"Hamburg, Germany," I replied.

"Your nationality?"

"Polish," I replied.

"How is that possible when you were born in Germany?"

"My parents were Polish nationals living in Germany, and I also held a Polish passport since birth," I responded.

"That does not seem likely; can you prove it?"

"I was born in Hamburg, Germany, but held a Polish passport, like my parents, since birth. I spent the war years in Poland, but after Auschwitz I was left without documents of any kind."

"You were born in Germany, and that, in our eyes, makes you a German national."

"Maybe in your eyes, but I'm not a German. I always had Polish papers." Being Polish was not such a bargain, I thought to myself, but it was infinitely better than being German.

The two officers thanked me politely, got up, and left the office. I was worried about losing my job. Had I given the right answers?

Several weeks later, Fred called from Holland. He sounded

upset and disappointed. "My application to marry you has been rejected. No reason was given. I am angry and so very, very sorry."

I was crushed. My plan had failed. But in the back of my mind, there was also a tiny speck of relief—I wouldn't have to marry Fred.

The next morning I entered Major Brinton's office.

"Old girl, you blew it!" he burst out. "Remember those two officers who came to interview you?"

"Who are you talking about?" I was confused.

"The two who inquired about your background, nationality, etc."

"Oh, yes, what about them?"

"Having been born in Germany was totally unacceptable to them. Your application for marriage was denied on those grounds. You cannot marry a British soldier."

I was speechless and angry. Had I known, I would have doctored my story. There were no papers to prove anything. I could have said that I had been born in Poland. But it was too late now.

Major Brinton, seeing me close to tears, changed the subject. "Tell me about yourself. I know very little about you. How did you happen to wind up here?"

"I was shipped by the Germans from Hamburg to the Lodz ghetto and lived and worked there under horrible conditions. I lost my mother and sister there. My father had been killed six months earlier in Dachau. As the Russian army advanced, the Germans liquidated the ghetto and shipped us to Auschwitz. From there I was transferred to Neuengamme-Dessauer Ufer, Neuengamme-Sasel, and at the end to Bergen-Belsen."

"What kind of work did you do in those places?"

"Mostly office work, some construction, manual labor, and factory work."

"Please be a little more specific about the work," Major Brinton insisted.

"At Dessauer Ufer, we slept in the old warehouse on hard floors, and during the day we worked at shipyards, various construction sites, and bombed-out factories, performing hard physical labor—mainly the clearing of bomb damage with our bare hands. At Neuengamme-Sasel, it was a different story. Word got around on the first day that I spoke and wrote German. I was assigned to the office along with another woman. There I kept records on the distribution of food items and daily updated the roster both for inmates of the camp and for the SS guards, including their names and addresses. The work became so routine that after several weeks I could recite all forty-two names and addresses of the SS personnel. I often wondered what good this would do. I never believed that I would survive the war."

"Did you really memorize the SS names and addresses?" Major Brinton sounded incredulous.

I nodded my head. "Every one of them. Why do you ask?"

"They are war criminals." He sounded excited. "You must see Colonel Tilling at War Crimes with this information tomorrow. I'll call ahead and tell him to expect you."

I thought about how difficult it might be to talk about the Germans, to relive the past. Major Brinton sensed my reluctance.

"I see you're reconsidering, Celia. But you must go. You owe it to those who suffered and died. Promise me you'll go."

I promised.

At 9:00 the following morning, my fingers rested on the doorknob of Colonel Tilling's office. The sign on the door read:

J. H. Tilling
Lt-Colonel RA
Comd No 1 War Crimes Investigation Team
Hohne (Belsen) Camp

I was not sure that I really wanted to get further involved, but I remembered my promise to Major Brinton and opened the door. I found Colonel Tilling sitting behind his desk. He was a man of slight build, with short-cropped reddish hair, a small mustache, and the bluest eyes I had ever seen. He looked up.

"Can I help you?" he asked.

"I'm not sure. Major Brinton suggested that I come to see you," I replied.

"Oh, yes, I received Jock's phone call. He told me that you have information of interest to War Crimes. Please start at the beginning."

I took a deep breath and started my story. "From September 1944 to March 1945, just prior to my coming to Bergen-Belsen, I was an inmate of the Neuengamme concentration camp and worked at two of its work camps, Arbeitslager Dessauer Ufer and Arbeitslager Sasel near Hamburg."

Colonel Tilling listened attentively.

"During the last six months, I worked in the Sasel camp office and memorized the names and addresses of the forty-two SS men and women who guarded us."

Colonel Tilling looked at me questioningly, then handed me a pad and pencil. "Please write all of them down."

I could sense that he was waiting to be convinced.

"Tell me," he continued, before I could start writing, "are there any other witnesses who can corroborate your statements?"

"Yes, there are," I replied, "several friends: Elli Sabin, who is now in the hospital, and two others who share my room, Hela Dimand and Sabina Zarecki."

I thought about our time together in Sasel, how I had worked indoors while Elli and Sabina had worked outdoors. I would frequently show them the welts and bruises that Kommandant Stark inflicted daily on my legs and face. For no apparent reason, he would vent his anger and frustration on me and my coworker by beating and kicking our shins with his hobnailed boots. I would certainly not forget to put Kommandant Stark's name on the list.

Starting with the letter A, I began to write down all forty-two names. But when I got to the end of the list, I felt unsure about one of the SS.

"Colonel Tilling," I began, "there is one Wachtmeister I have a question about. He was the lowest possible SS grade, the rank of Rottenführer. He was dismissed or transferred about two months before the end of the war due to a bleeding ulcer. Do I include him in the list or not?"

"Is there anything else you recall about him?" Colonel Tilling wanted to know.

I nodded. "I'll tell you the story if you're interested."

"Of course, I need as much information as I can get," he answered.

This SS guard was short, I told Colonel Tilling, with a pale face, washed-out blond hair, and almost colorless blue eyes. He answered to the name of Wolfgang. His guard duty was mostly at the main gate, which divided the camp inside from the SS barracks outside. Often he'd march up and down outside our office window trying to keep warm. Sometimes, when he felt he was unobserved, he'd slow his steps and look through the window. Occasionally, he'd smile and even venture a whispered hello. He seemed strange—the only one of the forty-two SS guards who didn't shout at us or beat us.

I decided to try and talk to him about an escape plan. The next time I saw him outside the office, I took my box of paper clips, opened the door, dropped the box, and bent down to pick the clips up, one by one.

He whispered a guarded hello and told me that he had heard that I used to live in Hamburg and that he had lived in Altona-Luna Park. I had never been there, but I recalled that it was a poor area with mostly tenement houses and dark dismal flats.

He told me that he was not like the other SS, that before Hitler he had been a member of the Communist party. I was very surprised and looked at him with renewed interest. He might be just another "parlor Communist," I thought, but perhaps he would help me escape. I decided I'd take a chance on him.

I summoned my courage and asked in a low voice if he would let me escape and find a place for me to hide. He looked terrified! Then he asked if I knew the penalty for both of us if we were caught. But I was determined and decided to try a bribe. I told him I had inherited some houses in Altona and offered to write one of the houses over to him. After the war, he would be a rich man. His eyes danced with interest, but he quickly turned and walked away.

Three weeks later, he entered the office, pointed at me,

handed me a sack, and commanded that I pick up the trash near the outside gate. I did as I was told while he walked close behind me. He said he had gone to the Stadthaus, had checked the real estate registers, and knew I had told the truth. He said that he was a poor man and a house would mean a lot. But he made no commitment. I could only hope that his greed would convince him to help me carry out my plan.

For the next few weeks, Wolfgang avoided me, and I assumed that my proposition, while tempting, was too great a risk for him. Then, a few months after our conversation, Wolfgang disappeared completely. I began to worry that he might denounce me. Finally, early one morning, the Oberscharführer came to my desk and shouted that Rottenführer Wolfgang had been discharged due to a bleeding ulcer and was to be deleted from the roster. I never saw him again.

When I finished this story, Colonel Tilling was silent for a moment, then said, "Put Wolfgang's name on the list for the time being."

I added the name and handed him the list. He scanned it silently for a few moments and then looked at me. "Tell me, why did it take you more than three months to come forward and give us this list?"

"I had no idea that you would be interested or that you would take any action. I had given up any hope of arrests or a trial, any hope of justice at all."

"Girl, are you crazy? Of course there will be justice. I'll just need a few days to check all of this out."

We shook hands, and I left his office thinking of the Germans, seeing their faces, remembering . . . Would I see them behind bars? Would they stand trial? Would they be convicted? I had my doubts. . . . But I did not have to wonder for very long, as I soon became involved in the interrogation of a high-ranking German official.

In mid-September, Major Brinton called me into his office. "Cecilia, that was Captain Shelton on the telephone. He needs a team of interrogators and a translator. Seems that they have caught a fish of some importance. Tell Captain Murray and Sergeant Smith to come along, and the three of you meet me downstairs in the Jeep."

The ride to Hannover took no more than an hour. We discussed the prospect of catching the important German "fish" and decided that it would be more easily said than done. We'd already had some false alarms and hoped that this trip would be more worthwhile.

We parked the Jeep in front of a gray building and walked inside. We were led into a large room, light and airy in spite of the dirty windowpanes. The walls were pale green, and paint peeled off the long-neglected ceiling. The top of a white, ball-like lamp in the room was covered with black dust. We sat at a long table with four chairs, facing a huge, empty space. The door opened and two MPs led a German into the room. He was clad in slacks, a blue shirt, a gray windbreaker, and hiking boots. The German remained standing, facing us, hands straight at his sides in an almost military posture. He was tall, blond, with grayish eyes, probably no more than forty-five. He seemed very sure of himself and totally without fear. There was an air of defiance in the way his head was thrown back; an arrogant smirk played over his face. He looked at me, the only other civilian in the room. His lips curled into a cynical smile, as if he sensed the ironic reversal of our roles.

I couldn't help remembering when I had first begun to hate the Germans; it was the day that the two SS had come to take my father to Dachau. The feeling had frightened me then. That I had been capable of sustaining the intensity of this hatred surprised me now. I wondered if the German sensed it.

Major Brinton started with his usual questions. "Your name?"

"Günther Hoffmann."

"Rank and serial number?"

"Feldwebel, number 121416118."

"Unit of service: Luftwaffe, Wehrmacht, or SS?"

"Wehrmacht."

After I translated each question, the German answered slowly, deliberately.

"And you were stationed where?"

I barely had enough time to translate when the German replied, "Wehrmacht, Hungary."

"Sounds like a nice, safe answer to me—just a member of the regular army?"

"Yes, sir."

"Do you understand English?"

"No!"

"Then why did you say Wehrmacht before Hungary? Your answer came even before we had translated the question."

The German shrugged his shoulders.

"Let's go back to Hungary," said the major. "What did an officer of the Wehrmacht do in Hungary?"

"Orders—I went where I was sent. I was a soldier."

"How long were you in Hungary?"

"Six months."

"And after that?"

"Transferred."

He was not going to make it easy for us. He did not volunteer a single word.

"Transferred where?"

"Back to Berlin."

His answer hit a nerve. Berlin, the place where orders were issued. Berlin, the seat of Himmler's death machine.

"What did you do in Berlin?"

"Just army clerical work."

"Tell us more—specifics, details, etc."

"There is nothing else to tell. I was a soldier and followed orders."

"We seem to have reached a dead end," the major said, turning toward us. "He does not want to talk to us!"

The German stood erect, still smirking. He knew we were in the dark.

"I am known as a patient man, but at this moment I am very angry!" Major Brinton shouted.

His next move seemed to have been drawn from some prewar courtroom strategy. He took from his briefcase a bottle of Scotch, cups, chocolate, biscuits, several packs of Player cigarettes, and matches. "Let's take a break, drink, smoke, and wait. We have lots of time!"

Slowly, Major Brinton poured the drinks. We lit cigarettes, smoked, talked, and laughed, ignoring the German. We would take a few drags on our cigarettes, then squash them in ashtrays, only to light other ones. We opened biscuits and chocolates and began to eat them. The German standing in front of us was mesmerized and eyed the snacks enviously. I felt no pity; I remembered how I'd spent the last six months of the war in Auschwitz and Bergen-Belsen reduced to a creature with a shaven head, a little water, and some thin, watery soup.

Three hours passed; I was tiring, but Major Brinton was ready to resume.

"Let's go back to Berlin. Where did you work and for whom? And why Wehrmacht? Are you absolutely sure?"

"Yes, I am sure," said the German, but he no longer sounded convincing. "Definitely not SS," he said.

The major's outward calm belied his rage. His eyes were blazing, but he remained in control. I admired the man. I looked at the German, his eyes shifting hungrily from the cigarette smoke to the half-smoked butts in the ashtray. He was wetting his lips. Surely, he was a smoker and this was painful for him.

For me, the smoke evoked the more painful memory of the black clouds that billowed from the chimneys at Auschwitz and the stench that polluted the air when the crematorium was working overtime. Once again I heard the camp orchestra playing Beethoven and saw myself standing in the Appellplatz watching long lines of human beings struggle silently to their deaths. Before this nightmare could engulf me, I abruptly pulled myself back to the green room.

The German was becoming nervous and fidgety. He could no longer stand completely still. I sensed that Major Brinton was about to play his next card; I had seen him make this move before. His voice was sweet and calm, almost gentle.

"We have wasted hours on you, and since you really do not want to cooperate, we will turn you over to the Russians in Berlin. They have other ways of dealing with you. Or . . ."

His voice trailing off, he turned and looked at me. I stared at the German.

The German trembled. He no longer smiled. Several minutes passed and finally, stammering and stuttering, he gave us our answers.

"I was an Obersturmbannführer in the SS stationed at Oranienburg concentration camp—but I'm innocent. I only followed orders." He was perspiring. "It was a work camp, and only those who died were cremated there."

"I understand. You bastards just worked your prisoners till they dropped dead, and then you cremated their bodies. You call that civilized?" The major's face was red with anger. The room seemed to be getting smaller, and I felt a stabbing pain in the back of my head. I wanted to scream. The major muttered, "Damn bloody bastard."

Slowly and deliberately, he removed his revolver from its holster. He carefully released the safety and placed it on the table in front of me. I looked questioningly at the major, then at the weapon. The butt was made of dark wood, the barrel of gleaming black steel. Major Brinton shifted his gaze between me and the revolver in silent suggestion. I picked up the gun with a steady hand and, without hesitation, pointed it at the German.

All during the war I had wished for a gun. I had wanted to kill one German—just one—before I died. Seconds passed; the revolver was heavy and trembled in my hand. The German's eyes avoided mine, but his lips quivered an almost inaudible "please."

I closed my eyes. Almost immediately I heard my father's voice reaching me from Dachau where they had murdered him: "If you let yourself hate too long and too much, it will destroy you in the end."

I put the revolver down, placing it on the table in front of Major Brinton, and walked to the door. Outside in the hallway, I sank slowly to the floor and leaned against the cold wall, remembering . . . remembering. I was confronted with a cruel irony: somehow I still could not justify killing another human being; somehow, I had retained my faith in a just system of courts and juries.

This incident strengthened my decision to continue my involvement with Colonel Tilling's plan to locate and arrest the former SS. But I was not convinced that he had taken me seriously until, just a few days later, a Jeep driven by a corporal pulled up in front of the barracks. The corporal asked for me by name. "Please come with me; Colonel Tilling wants to talk to you."

I grabbed my jacket and got into the Jeep. As we entered Colonel Tilling's office, he jumped up. "Good morning! It's good of you to come on such short notice. Your data and all the information you gave me checked out. I also heard that you know the city of Hamburg. I'd like you to come along when we take a lorry and pick the bastards up, even the coward Wolfgang."

The thought of returning to Hamburg, the city where I had lived with my parents, terrified me. It meant facing the memories of my childhood and the pain of my loss, and it meant facing the Germans once again. But I was also curious, and I agreed before I allowed myself to realize fully what all this might mean.

"How about next Monday?" asked Colonel Tilling. "The

team will consist of four officers, a driver, and you. We'll pick you up at 8:00 in the morning. OK?"

"That's fine. I'll be ready. But what's going to happen? What will I have to do?"

"Wait and see. You won't be disappointed."

Monday morning, exactly at 8:00, they picked me up. The officers introduced themselves. We chatted and smoked during the two-hour ride from Bergen-Belsen to Hamburg. As we entered the city limits, the familiar streets awakened both pain and anger. I had come back—alone. Fortunately, I had little time to think about it.

The British pulled out a carefully marked map, and the officer in charge began explaining, "You go up first. We don't want to scare the Germans into hiding. Ring the bell, and ask, in German, for the former SS. We'll be right behind you, quiet and invisible. If he or she is home, we'll take over. If not, find out when they'll be back, thank them politely, and leave. But we'll return. Understood?"

"Yes, sir."

We made our first stop at an old, working-class tenement building. My heart was pounding as I climbed the stairs and came to a stop in front of a door marked "Müller." I pushed the bell, and a shrill noise pierced the air. An old man appeared at the door.

"Ist Frau Müller zu Hause? Ich möchte sie sehen," I asked.

"Irma, jemand hier für Dich!" he shouted.

From the back room I heard her only too familiar voice, "Ich komme sofort."

A few seconds later, we stood face to face. She looked

horrified, too stunned to talk or ask the reason for my visit. I, too, was speechless, remembering the beatings that had left thick welts on my face. I stood frozen with fear and was relieved to hear the footsteps of the British officers. They stood behind me, their hands resting on their sidearms.

"Come with us!" one of them said to Mrs. Müller. She looked at us, seemingly in a state of shock, not moving.

"Please translate into German," the officer requested as he turned toward me. I repeated his sentence in German. As she shouted her response, I translated her lies into English.

"I was always fair and decent," she screamed. "I never did anything unless they deserved it." Pointing at me, she yelled, "She can confirm it!"

I instinctively backed away in fear, anticipating that she would hit me again. Then I remembered that I was in the company of the British.

"That's almost funny!" I replied. "You used to beat us without mercy. You were a sadistic, cruel beast ..." I choked on my words and turned away. It was over; I'd done it. Although I told myself there was no longer any reason to be afraid, the old fears persisted.

Back in the truck, Mrs. Müller was under guard, sitting on a bench in the flatbed. The British continued their search, not bothering to ask me whether I was tired or not. They had a job to do. We proceeded from one German to the next, each time repeating the same process: SS Paasch, SS Piertz, SS Himmel, and so on. It gradually became easier for me, especially as all of the Germans, men and women alike, repeated that they were without guilt. They claimed that they had done nothing wrong—only followed orders.

By 6:00 P.M., we had turned seventeen Germans over to a

military prison in Hamburg. The next morning and each succeeding morning, we returned to the streets in search of others until we had taken forty prisoners. The two names remaining on my list were the former commandants, now living in southern Germany. They were to be brought north by the Americans.

On our last day, we took a lunch break. We needed a walk, a change, and some relaxation. A drizzly rain fell on our raincoats. As we walked through the streets of downtown Hamburg, which had been badly bombed during the war, I remembered it as it had looked years ago.

"This area used to be fashionable, with elegant stores and a beautiful lake," I explained. We walked along Jungfernstieg, turning the corner into Neuer Wall and continuing up the street. We strolled along, chatting and laughing, blocking the sidewalk, but we didn't care. Striding toward us, heading in the opposite direction, was a young man. He was dressed in a trench coat, a matching cap, and under his arm he carried a briefcase. We gave him room on the sidewalk so he could pass, and as he came alongside our group, our eyes met for one brief second. We instantly recognized each other, but before I could utter his name, he ran down the street and disappeared around the corner.

"Anyone you know?" the major inquired.

"No," I lied, although now I knew that Leonard Luft, the former head of the ghetto Labor Department, had survived the war.

Luft had drawn up deportation lists for the Germans, he had thrown me out of his office when I had begged for a job, and he had been generally detested by all. I thought briefly about revenge. But I couldn't denounce him. He was, after all, a Jew. I wondered whether his past haunted him, if he was able to live with his conscience. Then I remembered that his actions hadn't bothered him in the ghetto, and I surmised that they wouldn't bother or change him now. There was nothing to be gained from pursuing him.

A week later, Colonel Tilling called me to his office. "Thank you. You've been of great help. Anything I can do for you?" he wanted to know.

My reply was immediate and urgent. "I want desperately to get out of Germany! Can you help me?"

"I can try, but there isn't much I can do." He sounded sorry. "Anything else?"

"Yes. When you have all forty-two SS in custody and behind bars, I'd like to walk past their cells, to see them in prison, while I am free."

He nodded. "I understand. Next week we'll take you. We're still interrogating and getting statements. And I'll need your story as well."

"I'll write it down for you; if you have additional questions, please let me know."

"Good, thanks again." He made no mention of a trial date, and I assumed my work was finished.

A week later, when I returned with my detailed statement, the corporal was expecting me. I felt safer now, although still not secure. The fear of the past several years was not easily dispelled.

"We have orders to take you to the military stockade on Thursday," said the corporal. "We'll fetch you at 9:00 in the morning."

Exactly at 9:00, several British officers in a Jeep picked me up. Their faces showed no curiosity, and I assumed that they had been briefed. I smoked and thought about the past. For a moment, I appreciated the miracle that I had lived to see my torturers caught. But then I was suddenly besieged by an overwhelming anger at what the Germans had done: the suffering; the humiliation; the thousands, millions of Jews, including my family—all dead. Not even justice would suffice.

We arrived at the prison that had been used by the Germans before the war. It probably had housed Jews, political dissidents, and others the Germans had labeled "undesirable." Now it was filled with German SS and guarded by British soldiers. The officers led me down a flight of stairs to a block of ordinary prison cells. The iron bars left enough space so that I could see their faces clearly. They stood, each and every one, pressing their angry faces against the bars, watching. They recognized me as I walked down the long corridor past their cells. "Please help us!" some of them cried out. "We never did any harm!"

I couldn't respond. I looked at their pinched faces, the arrogance gone, and kept on walking. I felt no joy—only hatred and contempt for them and those like them who had reduced us to animals. As we approached the end of the cell block, the door was opened for us, and we stepped outside. It was warm and sunny, and the fresh air brought a sense of relief. I wanted to forget, to get away, to leave Germany forever and put the Germans out of my mind. I had to find a way.

Weeks later, Colonel Tilling called and left word for me to come to his office. What could they want now?

"Thanks for coming. The hearing is scheduled in a military court in Celle, about thirty kilometers from here, in October. We'll need you as a witness," he said.

I thought I had finished with the Germans. Turning them in was one thing, testifying still another. Despite the dread of facing them one more time, I knew that I had to finish what I had started. I knew I was safe, yet my fear remained.

"Let me know when, and I'll be there," I replied. My voice sounded firm, but I wanted to turn and run.

"I knew you wouldn't let me down!" He smiled and sounded relieved.

The day finally arrived. The ride from Bergen-Belsen to Celle was uneventful. I wore a dark suit and a white blouse that I had "purchased" with cigarettes sent by friends in Great Britain and the United States. A single cigarette on the black market was worth the equivalent of one mark; a carton had convinced a tailor to make me a new suit. It was a drastic change from my ragged, striped prison dress.

When we entered the municipal building in Celle, I was taken to a room and asked to wait. I sat silently, chain-smoking, hands shaking, unable to concentrate. Finally, the door opened and someone called my name. Mechanically, I followed a British uniform into the courtroom, dimly noticing several British officers sitting at a long, dark brown table. Their faces were unfamiliar. My eyes skimmed the row of Germans, now in civilian dress and guarded by military police. I tried to avoid looking at them.

"Please state your name," an officer behind the long table requested. I assumed that he was the British prosecutor.

"Cecilia Landau," I replied.

"Do you wish to speak German or English?"

"English, please," I answered.

The room was hot and stuffy, and I started to perspire. My head was throbbing; I began to lose all sense of self and time. I was oblivious to my surroundings. I saw only the Germans, the former SS, sitting in front of me, their faces contorted with hate. I can remember hearing the prosecutor's voice, but I can't recall either his questions or my answers. It was as if I were in a vacuum. I felt nothing until a hand touched my arm and led me out to the waiting Jeep.

"Come, we'll drive you back," said Colonel Tilling as he steadied me. "Thank you," he continued. "You were a great help."

I nodded but felt no satisfaction or joy. In the days that followed, I tried to recall the details of the hearing, but I could not.

Several weeks later, Sabina burst into the room. "Have you heard? The verdict is in! Prison sentences from two to twenty years for forty of them. Two, the commandant, who had beaten a woman to death, and one other, a high-ranking SS man, are sentenced to death."

So it was over, done. I thought that perhaps now I might be able to feel some satisfaction, some happiness, but there was still only relief and sadness.

My nights were long and black, and sleep came only for short periods at a time. What had been a reality in the past now repeated itself in recurring nightmares: German boots chasing me through the dark of the night, flashlights searching me out. The horrors remained vivid and alive. I saw the camps, my parents, my sister, and their drawn, fearful faces. Then there was the guilt: I was alive; they were not. With much effort, I kept going, one day at a time. If only I could leave . . .

Weeks passed and I was still without a plan. I was rapidly losing patience with the HIAS and its promises. Although my friends seemed resigned to waiting, I was obsessed with leaving and decided to find some way out *now*.

Early in December, I found a scribbled note that had been pushed under our barracks door. It was addressed to me. In large letters, it said, "Dreckjude, wir werden Dich finden. Du wirst nicht lange leben." Signed: SS.

I rushed to Colonel Tilling's office with the note and threw it on his desk. He asked me to translate: "Filthy Jew, we will find you. You won't live long."

His response was immediate but cool and calm. "Don't worry, it's probably just a crank note from a child of one of the convicted SS."

"How do you know that they won't come looking for me?"

"Don't worry, I'll have it checked out."

I left his office angry, knowing that Colonel Tilling still didn't realize that the Germans were capable of anything. Would the British be able to protect me? Once again, I started looking over my shoulder. A week later, I found a second note, almost identical to the first. By the time I reached Colonel Tilling's office, I was hysterical. Tears of anger, frustration, and helplessness streamed down my face. For some inexplicable reason, I was more afraid now than I had been during the war.

Colonel Tilling looked at the note on his desk.

"What now?" I sobbed.

"I think the time has come for you to leave here."

Leave—really leave? Could it be true?

Colonel Tilling picked up the telephone and requested

that Captain Alexander join us. I had met the captain briefly at the officers' club.

A few minutes later he entered.

"We have to get her out of Germany," Colonel Tilling said, "immediately. Weren't you taking three other women to Belgium?"

"Yes, we have made plans. We can leave as soon as you wish. But we need documents to cross borders, the proper papers for a staff car, and anything else that might make crossing out of Germany into Holland, Belgium, and France easier."

Colonel Tilling looked at Captain Alexander, then at me. "We'll arrange for the documents. I hope they'll get you to Paris. There you'll have a chance to obtain either a certificate to Palestine or a visa for the United States. Be ready in two days."

Slowly, I walked back to my room, the joy of my immediate reaction diminishing as I thought of leaving the only friends I had, of being alone in a strange place, and of possible impending danger. I thought of the combinations of choice and fate that had brought me to this point: it was ironic that the hearing and the resulting death threats from my enemies had finally accomplished just what I had wanted all along.

Out of the Ashes ∿

1945–1956

I had two days to get ready. I packed two small cardboard satchels with the sparse belongings I had acquired at Bergen-Belsen during the eight months since liberation: a pair of shoes, a few cosmetics, some underwear, a suit, an extra skirt, and several blouses. All the cigarettes I had received from friends abroad, I had traded for clothing. I decided to wear my herringbone coat for the trip. Silently and sadly, my roommates, Hela and Sabina, watched me pack. Ever since liberation, they had watched me plot and scheme to leave Germany. Now, not only was this happening but my luck seemed to be changing as well. Shortly after the British had arranged for my departure, my former schoolmate, Lottie Strauss, and her husband, Herb, now living in New York, had located me through the International Red Cross. They had promised to send an affidavit for me. I should have been ecstatic.

Instead, I discovered to my surprise that it was difficult, almost painful, to leave the friends I had made over the past four years. We had, after all, shared experiences that few others could ever understand: the camps, the loss of loved

ones, the deaths, the hunger, the beatings, the dehumanization, and, finally, liberation.

There was a knock on our door. The corporal who worked
for Colonel Tilling entered and addressed me: "Please come
to the office with me now. There are some documents waiting for you."

I quickly wiped my tears and followed him out.

Colonel Tilling sat down at his desk. As he handed me the
envelope, he said, "This letter will explain your special situation to anyone in Paris, that you were of help to us here at
British War Crimes, and that for your own protection, you
must be able to go abroad. I am sure that when the American authorities in Paris read the letter, they will help. Now
please come with me to the adjacent office. We'll give you
the permit you need to enter France. But we cannot provide
the necessary papers to cross the Dutch border. We'll have to
count on a little luck."

As we entered, a young lieutenant stood up, saluted, and
then handed me a document written in French, with an
official-looking seal. This was to pass for an entry visa to
France. At the bottom was his signature: H. François-Poncet.
Colonel Tilling explained that the name was well known in
France. The young lieutenant was the son of a French cabinet member, and his name might prove useful. I thanked
him, and we all shook hands.

The following morning, a large, dark green staff car with
British markings was waiting in front of our barracks. Once
again there were tearful embraces. My friends watched as I
got into the car. A corporal was at the wheel and next to him
sat Captain Alexander. I joined three other young women in
the backseat. The captain immediately told us to call him

**No: 1 BRITISH WAR CRIMES
INVESTIGATION TEAM**

Subject: War Criminals   CONFIDENTIAL

TO WHOM IT MAY CONCERN:
————————————————

Cecelia LANDAU

1.   The above named is the chief witness against
aoma seventy war criminals wanted in connection with war crimes
at SASEL Concentration Camp, near HAMBURG.

2.   Several families of these persons wanted for
orimes are at present living in HAMBURG, and information has
reached this office that these families have expressed their
intention of avenging themselves on, among others, Cecelia LANDAU.

3.   As a result of these threats and the fact that
fourteen accused persons were acquitted at the BELSEN trials and
two Hungarians were also acquitted at a trial at CELLE, I understand
that Cecelia LANDAU has become ill with worry over her position here.

4.   I understand that she has received affidavits
enabling her to go to AMERICA. In the circumstances, may I
request whoever it may concern to expedite Cecelia LANDAU's
departure from BELSEN, and advise that if it is possible she
should be allowed to proceed immediately to PARIS to await transport
to the USA.

5.   This request is made not only for her own sake
but because the presence of such a person in BELSEN will have
the effect of making other potential witnesses unwilling to come
forward to give evidence which is required urgently in order that
other suspected criminals may be brought to trial.

J.H. Fielding

Lt-Colonel RA
Comd No 1 War Crimes Investigation Team

c/o HQ 4 Wilts
HOHNE (BELSEN) Camp
————————————
12 Dec 45

Alex. We introduced ourselves: Beatrice from Brussels; Anita and Renate, sisters, formerly from Breslau. We chatted excitedly about the prospect of finally leaving Germany, none of us able to believe that it was really happening. Anita lovingly cradled a cello.

"I played in the orchestra at Auschwitz," she volunteered, "and I plan to be a concert performer." I admired her self-assurance in determining her future. Although I had hopes of a job, marriage, children, and a normal life, I was beset by many doubts.

We drove all morning and most of the afternoon through Germany toward Holland. The countryside gradually became more inhabited; occasional farms dotted the landscape.

"Be quiet now," Alex whispered. "We're almost at the Dutch border. They may have some questions about civilians without passports. I'll do all the talking."

I shuddered at the thought of being turned back and having to return to the displaced persons' camp. The border guards saw us approaching and shouted, "HALT!" Our car came to an abrupt stop. Alex rolled down the window and produced a wad of documents. The Dutch guard examined them carefully, one piece of paper at a time, and then summoned a senior officer. After further examination, the senior officer addressed the captain.

"Sorry, old chap, can't let you pass with these civilians. These military papers are not valid for entry by nonmilitary personnel. Civilians need passports and Dutch visas."

"These civilians are under the protection of the British military government," Alex said in a firm voice. "You have to let us pass."

The Dutch guards were not impressed. Alex argued and

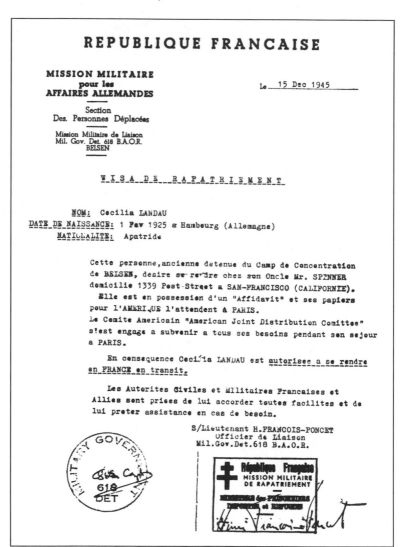

REPUBLIQUE FRANCAISE

MISSION MILITAIRE
pour les
AFFAIRES ALLEMANDES

Le ___15 Dec 1945___

Section
Des. Personnes Déplacées

Mission Militaire de Liaison
Mil. Gov. Det. 618 B.A.O.R.
BELSEN

V I S A   D E   R A P A T R I E M E N T

NOM: Cecilia LANDAU
DATE DE NAISSANCE: 1 Fev 1925 à Hambourg (Allemagne)
NATIONALITE: Apatride

Cette personne, ancienne detenue du Camp de Concentration
de BELSEN, desire se rendre chez son Oncle Mr. SPINNER
domicilie 1339 Pest-Street a SAN-FRANCISCO (CALIFORNIE).
Elle est en possession d'un "Affidavit" et ses papiers
pour l'AMERIQUE l'attendent à PARIS.
Le Comite Americain "American Joint Distribution Comittee"
s'est engage a subvenir a tous ses besoins pendant son sejour
a PARIS.

En consequence Cecilia LANDAU est autorisee a se rendre
en FRANCE en transit.

Les Autorites Civiles et Militaires Francaises et
Allies sont priees de lui accorder toutes facilites et de
lui preter assistance en cas de besoin.

S/Lieutenant H.FRANCOIS-PONCET
Officier de Liaison
Mil.Gov.Det.618 B.A.O.R.

République Française
MISSION MILITAIRE
DE RAPATRIEMENT

pleaded and finally threatened. It seemed hopeless. Then he turned to his driver and hissed something under his breath. Suddenly the corporal put the car into reverse, revved the engine, shot backward, then turned and sped down an embankment, through a dried-up creek, and up a hillside. We could hear the Dutch guards yelling.

"Hit the floor!" Alex shouted. "The bastards are raising their guns!" We crouched on the floor, frightened, while the car sped on. Five minutes later, Alex told us we could get up. We had lost sight of the Dutch guards. In the front seat, Alex heaved a sigh of relief.

"Too close for comfort," he murmured. The back of his neck was wet with perspiration. Somewhere, we had managed to cross the border into Holland, and although we were apprehensive, we asked no questions.

It was early evening when we stopped at the Belgian border. Here, the guards paid little attention to us and waved us on without a question. Two hours later we were approaching Brussels. Vivid red, blue, and yellow neon lights danced and sparkled in the distance. Minutes later, we were in the city amid people, stores, heavy traffic, and the bustle of normal life. We had not seen cities like this since before the war and had completely forgotten that they existed. We felt like little children in a fairy tale, and we began to laugh and sing.

Our driver stopped in front of an old, stately apartment building. Alex informed us that we'd be staying the night with Mr. and Mrs. Lazarus, friends of his parents. We climbed the stairs to the third floor and rang the bell. Mrs. Lazarus cautiously opened the door, but a smile spread across her face when she saw Alex—and the cartons of K rations he carried in his arms.

"We'll be here one night, my driver and I, and the four girls."

He began to introduce us, but Mrs. Lazarus interrupted, "Where are they from?"

"Bergen-Belsen," Alex replied.

"Oh, my God," she burst out, "they must be full of lice and disease. They'll have to sleep in the hall. I don't want them in the rooms."

The captain argued but could not persuade Mrs. Lazarus to change her mind. We did indeed sleep in the hall on the hard floorboards. We left in the morning before breakfast, dropping Beatrice off at her friend's house in Brussels and the two sisters at the home of their relatives. All would eventually make their way to their families in London.

Captain Alex, the driver, and I continued our journey. At the border crossing into France, the guards wanted to see my visa. I produced my entry permit signed by François-Poncet. The familiar name was sufficient to get us across the border. They waved us on, wishing us bon voyage. By evening we had reached Lille. Tired and hungry, we parked the car in the town square near a small restaurant, entered, and devoured the only item on the menu—a chicken dinner. Bread was still rationed and in short supply, the waiter explained, but he brought us three small pieces. The captain ordered some wine and a sticky, sweet dessert. A man sitting in the corner played the accordion while several couples danced.

"How about a dance?" Alex asked.

I smiled. I had liked him from the first time I'd seen him at the officers' club. He was good-looking, outgoing, and seemed fun-loving. But romantic notions had ended abruptly when I heard from one of his fellow officers that he was engaged to a girl in London. Now Alex and I danced a slow fox-trot.

"We'll drop you off at the railroad station and put you on the 10:00 train for Paris," he said. He had it all planned. We went back to the table, paid the bill, and walked outside. But our car was nowhere in sight. I was horrified, but Alex only laughed. "Stolen," he said. "C'est la vie!"

The satchel with all my clothing was gone! All those cigarettes—traded for nothing! All I had left now was the small case I had carried with me. Gradually, my initial panic dissolved into resignation. After all, the past years had always been like this—having things and losing them. There was nothing I could call my own.

We walked slowly to the railroad station where Alex bought my one-way ticket, third class, to Paris. He waited on the platform as I walked into the compartment and rolled down the window.

"Thanks for everything," I said. "I'll never forget it."

"Don't mention it."

"Please tell me one thing," I went on. "I just have to know why you were picked to drive us out of Germany... why you didn't just turn back at the Dutch border... why you cared ... why you took the risk."

"Haven't you guessed?" he asked, looking very serious. "I'm a Jew, like you, but I was lucky enough to have left Berlin for London in 1936."

The conductor blew his whistle, and the train began to inch forward. We shook hands through the open window. Alex stepped back, and I waved until my tear-filled eyes lost sight of him.

Sitting in the train, alone again, I realized that I had closed a chapter of my life and was about to begin a new one. As the train rambled through the dark French countryside, I began to doze. Perhaps now I could begin to put the past behind me. But as I listened to the clacking noise of the train, pictures of the German cattle cars that had transported us from camp to camp during the war flashed through my mind. They were always vile smelling and overcrowded, permeated with an atmosphere of anxiety, confusion, and sadness. Now I had an entire compartment to myself, and for the first time in five years I knew my own destination. I knew that when the train stopped, I would be in Paris.

At 4:00 A.M., the train came to a rolling halt.

"PARIS!" the conductor shouted.

Had I really made it? Could I really start a new life? I grabbed my bag and walked into the dimly lit waiting room of the station.

The room was deserted, with the exception of a couple of ragged men snoring in the corner. One look at the iron gate across the Métro entrance brought back another memory— this time of the iron gates and barbed wire of the camps. I was shaking. The sign above the Métro indicated that the gates would open at 6:00 A.M., a two-hour wait. I didn't dare walk outside in the dark, so I sat down on a long bench, placed the small satchel at my knees, and dozed fitfully. I awoke with a start when a British army lieutenant sat down next to me. We made some small talk, and he helped me locate the Jewish Youth Hostel at number 4, rue des Rosiers on his map. Finally, the guards appeared and opened the iron gates to the Métro. Downstairs, I caught the first train to the Saint Paul stop. Rue des Rosiers, number 4, was only a short walk from there.

I pressed the bell, and the door of the old gray building opened. The woman behind the desk looked at me. "What do you want?" she asked in French.

"The British sent me from Bergen-Belsen. I'm looking for a bed until I can obtain a visa for the United States," I replied in Yiddish, which was easier for me than French.

She studied a chart on her desk. "We're crowded, but I think I can find you a cot in the dormitory on the third floor. Follow me."

We climbed three flights of narrow stairs to a hallway that led to a large, darkened room. Inside there were thirty or forty cots, most of them occupied by sleeping women. At the end of the fourth row, she found an empty cot. "It's yours. Follow me and I'll show you the washroom."

I quickly dropped my satchel on the cot and followed her down the hall to a small, tiled room with a row of basins and spigots. "Auschwitz!" I thought immediately. But when I turned on one of the faucets, I noticed that here they had plenty of water. I wondered how long it would take to control the invasion of images from the past.

"Where are the showers?" I inquired.

"None," she answered. "You have to go to the bathhouse down the street, pay two francs, and they'll give you a towel and a hot tub to use for twenty minutes."

I was stunned. "And toilets?"

"Down three flights of stairs in the back courtyard are outhouses," she said matter-of-factly.

Life was not getting easier, after all, and I wondered if I'd ever be able to live in a normal place under normal conditions.

I walked back to the dormitory and sat down on the empty cot. The women had begun to get up. I introduced myself to the redhead who occupied the adjacent cot. Her name was Doris.

"Originally from Vienna," she said with a friendly smile, "but I came here from Bergen-Belsen several weeks ago." I recalled having seen her around the camp after liberation. "I'll show you around. We'll go to the American embassy to get you registered. It's a long, drawn-out procedure, and you'll have to stand in various lines from the moment you get there. They don't make it easy for us."

I nodded gratefully, but I was worried about money.

"How much does it cost to get there? I have just enough francs for two subway rides."

She looked me over carefully. "Don't worry, I have an idea. You won't need your black boots here. We can sell them easily, and the money will keep you afloat for some time. We don't need much, just Métro tickets and some francs for incidentals. We get one soup in the evenings at the hostel. It's really not too bad. Also, you'll get ration coupons, and then you can buy bread at the local bakery." She tried to sound cheerful.

It was a gray, overcast morning, but Paris had come to life. Stores were being opened, people were walking to work, gesticulating, chattering, and although their garments were worn, they seemed happy. The streets were wide and covered with freshly fallen snow. It did not, however, resemble the Paris of my dreams. I had thought of Paris as a city of fashionable people, of elegance. I had forgotten that here, too, the war and the German occupation would have left their mark.

As we walked to the subway, Doris pointed out important landmarks. We took the train to the Place de la Concorde. When we emerged from the underground, I noticed a mag-

nificent fountain in a square surrounded by old, stately buildings. Nothing seemed damaged here, as if the war had
bypassed this part of the city completely. The streets were
wide, and the trees, bare now, would be lush and green in the
spring.

We crossed the street to the front of the American embassy where a guard was trying to maintain some semblance
of order in the long line of people. Each person received a
slip of paper with a number on it, and we were told to wait
our turn. It was midafternoon by the time we entered the
building. Despite the cold weather, Doris waited patiently
with me. She had gone through the registration several
weeks earlier and knew the routine.

"Most likely," she said, "you'll have to come back daily
until you finally obtain a visa. They are slow and very par-
ticular about background information here."

I finally reached a desk staffed by a young clerk. I gave her
the slip of paper with the number, then my name. I asked if
the affidavit from my friends in New York had reached the
embassy. She checked her files and, much to my relief, informed me that it had arrived. She then handed me a long
list of other required documents: a health certificate—would
they notice that I had contracted TB during the war?—a
current passport—would the Poles be willing to issue one
to me?—a second affidavit—would my Uncle Adolf in San
Francisco send it? Even with the proper documents, I would
still need passage by boat to New York, and that had to be
paid for in advance. I still had lots of work to do!

After we left the embassy, Doris and I walked down the
wide boulevards and admired the old buildings. I remembered when Mother and I had been here for a few days in

1936 for the World's Fair. It had been a wonderful trip, and we had stayed at a luxurious hotel. Mother had been so happy. She spoke fluent French and loved the excitement of Paris. It all seemed so long ago—so much had happened since then. I forced myself to concentrate on the future.

Slowly and methodically, I began the process of acquiring the documents necessary for my departure to the United States. I wrote to Uncle Adolf in San Francisco for a second affidavit. I made repeated visits to the Polish embassy and requested a passport, which they repeatedly refused on the grounds that I had been born in Germany and did not speak flawless Polish. I went to the United States Lines Company, where they promised me passage on an empty merchant marine vessel if I could produce $600 and a visa for the United States. I wrote to Uncle Herschel in Palestine and asked if he could possibly send the $600. I promised to repay him once I started working.

For the next eight weeks, I went every morning, Monday through Friday, to the American embassy. I wanted to make sure that my name was still on the list and to see if I had received a German quota number. These were issued by place of birth. I was lucky; the German quota had not been used for more than four years, and I received a very low number. I also submitted Colonel Tilling's letter, which explained my work for the British War Crimes Department. The Americans seemed impressed and promised that as soon as I had taken care of all the formalities, they would issue the visa.

In the meantime, my visa to France expired. It had been issued as a transit visa for only two months, and the two months were up. But I needed more time to satisfy the requirements for the American authorities. I appealed to the prefecture for an extension but was repeatedly turned down. The possibility of being sent back to Germany loomed ominously in my mind. What could I do? I knew that "connections" were always helpful, but what connections did I have in France?

Then I remembered Léon Blum. A former French prime minister, he was supposedly the prisoner I had seen from the window of the infirmary in Neuengamme. Anyway, he was also a Jew, and he had been in a concentration camp. Perhaps he would be sympathetic toward someone who had been a fellow prisoner. It was worth a try.

It was not difficult to obtain his current address, and I took the Métro to a neighborhood with beautiful tree-lined streets and old stately apartment houses, in no way resembling the rue des Rosiers where I now lived. I found his building and walked up several flights of stairs. I rang the bell, and an elderly lady opened the door. In my poor French, I asked if I could please talk with Mr. Blum.

"Mr. Blum is sick. He can see no one," she replied.

"Please," I pleaded, "just say these two words to him: Auschwitz and Neuengamme!"

After a few moments, she returned. "He will see you, but don't stay long; it is too much for him."

I nodded.

She led me to the door at the end of a dimly lit hallway and opened it. The room was dark except for a small lamp on the desk. Behind the desk sat a white-haired gentleman, wearing a white shirt, a tie, and a dark jacket. He looked old and tired and seemed to be sick. I stood before him, awestruck.

"May I speak in German, Mr. Minister?" I asked timidly.

He gave a brief nod.

"My name is Cecilia Landau. The British drove me to France from Bergen-Belsen. I have applied for my visa to the United States, but meanwhile my transit visa has expired, and I cannot get it extended," I explained.

"Where did you spend the war?" he asked.

"Lodz ghetto, Auschwitz, Neuengamme, and Bergen-Belsen."

He looked at me silently, picked up the telephone, dialed a number, and spoke in a rapid French that I couldn't follow. When he finished, he turned to me. "It's OK. Return to the prefecture, ask for Mr. Rousseau, and you will receive your permit to stay."

I thanked him, shook his hand, and rushed back to the prefecture. The documents were ready and waiting. Just like the ghetto, I thought—you had to know someone to accomplish the impossible.

Some weeks later, at the beginning of February 1946, the affidavit from Uncle Adolf in San Francisco arrived. I also received the $600 from Uncle Herschel in Palestine. In the meantime, my health certificate was approved. Then, finally, my Polish passport was issued, but only after some trickery. In order to get it, I had been asked to produce a letter from someone who knew my father and could vouch that he was Polish. Getting this quickly seemed impossible, so I went to the Jewish Community Center to look for someone who would be willing to manufacture such a statement. A short, elderly gentleman volunteered, and although of course he had never known my father, he wrote the letter, had it typed up, and signed it. I thanked him for helping me play a joke on the Polish consulate.

The American embassy examined my collection of documents and promised to have a visa for me by the following week. On Tuesday morning, I returned once again, and I was called into the vice-consul's office. He produced a large document printed on heavy white paper. "The United States of America" was prominently printed at the top, followed by some small print and, finally, my name. At the bottom, there was a huge red seal with long red ribbons. The vice-consul handed it to me and wished me luck. Carefully, I put the large document into my shoulder bag and thanked him.

With the visa and $600 in hand, I rushed immediately to the United States Lines Company. After much haggling and pleading, I was assigned a berth on a merchant vessel headed for New York. I was told, "We are sailing from Bordeaux on March 4, on the SS *Anson Mills*. You'll have to be there in the morning with all your luggage and documents. The trip will take approximately twenty days."

I couldn't believe it! In a little more than twenty days, I would be in New York! I remembered my old friends, Julie and Julius, and could hear Julie's voice: "When you get to New York, remember to look for my son . . ."

After twenty-one days of seasickness, I stood on the deck of the *Anson Mills*, looking at the skyline of New York City. I was a long way, not only in miles, from the life I had known and the little girl I had been.

The boat docked near the Fulton Fishmarket, so the sign read, and the smell was enough to convince me. I buttoned my new brown coat and looked in my mirror. My hair was almost "long," barely covering my ears. I put on the beige pillbox hat I had bought in Paris and held tightly to my purse and my one small satchel. Finally, the gangplank was attached. I started down, scanning the crowd on the dock. There were Lottie and Herb, waiting for me. Their welcome was warm and kind, and I was happy.

A man stopped me. "New York News," he said.

I looked at Lottie.

"The press," she whispered.

"Will you please tell me where you come from and any other details you would care to share?"

I shook my head. I did not want to talk about the horrible past. "No comment," I replied and walked away.

We drove to Sunnyside, Long Island, where Lottie's parents, Mr. and Mrs. Rosenberg, lived. Before the war, they, too, had lived in Hamburg and had met my parents at the school that Lottie and I had attended. I would stay with them for the time being and sleep on their living room couch, which I made up every night as a bed. They were kind and sweet, but I quickly sensed their discomfort with my presence. They didn't quite know what to say to this "creature" from the concentration camps. Most of our time was spent in uneasy silence.

I spent the first few days in New York learning about the subway and bus systems. Occasionally, I took walks, even venturing onto Fifth Avenue, but I was easily frightened. It was too busy, too overwhelming. I felt like I had come from a small village. It would take time to get used to the pace here. America was so very different from anything I had known. Much to my surprise, I missed Europe. Although Lottie and I talked almost daily and saw each other on the weekends, I was lonely. Lottie and Herb were kind and hospitable, but we had different interests. I wanted to go to museums, to concerts. I was thinking of going back to school, but they thought I should be thinking about work and earning some money.

Then, barely two weeks after my arrival, the nightmares began. The horrors of the past that I had sometimes been able to suppress now found consistent expression in my dreams. Once again, I was running through the streets of Hamburg after dark, the Germans' flashlights searching for Mother and me. I was again lying face downward in the messy stink of the gutter. I could again hear their clicking boots coming closer...closer...closer...I would awake to the sound of my own screaming and the sight of Mr. and Mrs. Rosenberg standing next to my bed, speechless, frightened, and confused.

Perhaps it was just a coincidence, but shortly thereafter Lottie and her parents suggested that I find my own place. I looked around, but there were few vacancies in New York in 1946. I eventually found a small furnished room for $8 a week in a two-family building in Woodside. I was permitted to use the common bathroom and kitchen; sheets and towels were provided. Although I told myself over and over again how lucky I was, I felt forsaken in a strange land.

Now that I had a room, Lottie thought it absolutely essential that I find work as soon as possible. Herb was a salesman and Lottie designed sports items, but she had once worked in a glove factory in Queens. She contacted her old employer and arranged with him to take me on.

His small, storefront factory was located on the industrial side of Queens Boulevard in Sunnyside. The shop was crowded with women sewing leather gloves by hand. The pay was $1.25 per pair. If I hustled, I could finish seven pairs in a working day. At the end of the first week, my take-home pay after taxes was $28. After paying rent, buying food, and acquiring some American dresses, hardly anything was left. When I ran out of money, I would buy a candy bar for five cents and make that my noonday or evening meal.

Shortly after I started this first job, Lottie suggested that I apply for American citizenship and, at the same time, change my first name from Cecilia to Lucille. Lottie pointed out that my German and Polish nickname, "Cilli," would be pronounced "silly" in English. "Lucille sounds more American," she stated. I decided to follow her advice, but I kept Cecilia as my middle name.

Somehow, the weeks passed. I missed my friends in Europe, and finding new friends in New York was not easy. I had no contact with other young people and was too timid to make an effort. I wondered if life in New York would continue this way.

"Baruch ata Adonai . . ." Rose Rosenberg recited the blessings over the Shabbat candles. Her husband Max, at the opposite end of the table, smiled. It had been only eight weeks since my arrival in New York. I looked at the candles, the white tablecloth, the glistening china, and the challah in front of Max. The smiling faces around the table reminded me of Friday nights in my parents' house so many, many years ago. The past seemed distant, yet it had a way of becoming a presence, a part of the moment.

I looked at Rose and Max surrounded by their family. They were lucky. They had escaped Europe just two weeks before the onset of the war. Their son Howard and his wife Anne, as well as Lottie and her husband Herb, had come to celebrate the Friday night Shabbat dinner. Opposite me sat a young man, a friend of the family, I was told. He was about thirty, tall and slim, fair-skinned with blue eyes and short reddish hair. His features were even, almost symmetrical. He smiled. A nice, handsome face. He wore a brown suit, white shirt, and brown striped tie. He was somewhat quiet, but he seemed comfortable and knew everyone well.

"Lucille," Lottie began, "have you met Dan Eichengreen? He's Howard's former classmate from Hamburg, but he left Germany in 1939." The sound of the name sent shock waves through my body—it was the same as that of the friends I had met in the ghetto! Could this be the son that Julie and Julius had asked me to find in New York? Although the same name did not necessarily identify him as Julie's son, I couldn't deny my intuition. Sadly, I remembered my closeness to Julie, our tearful farewells, and my promise to look for her son if I got to New York before she did. I pushed the thought away. Even if it were true, I did not look forward to what lay ahead—telling him about his parents' deportation out of Lodz and their certain death. All through dinner, I was anxious, hoping that no one would bring up anything about me or my experiences during the war. No one did. But after everyone had left and Rose and I had cleared the table and begun the dishes, I felt I had to know for sure.

"Mrs. Rosenberg," I began cautiously, "did you know any of Dan's family?"

She looked surprised. "Why, yes, his parents often visited at our home."

"Do you have any vivid remembrances of them?"

"Yes, they were kind and intelligent, good company. But why these questions?"

"Tell me one more thing. Were their names Julie and Julius?"

"Yes, but why are you asking?"

Unable to respond, I dried the dishes in silence.

"Lucille," Mrs. Rosenberg persisted, "did you know them, too?"

"I was with them in the Lodz ghetto. We had traveled with them from Hamburg, and I grew very attached to them, especially Julie. We were close friends. But then they were deported out of the ghetto, and no one on their transport was ever heard from again."

Mrs. Rosenberg looked shocked.

"Do you think Dan knows? Have you talked to him?" she asked.

I shook my head. "I don't think I have the courage to confront him with such sad news."

Mrs. Rosenberg nodded, and nothing more was said.

Several weeks later, I met Dan again, this time at Lottie's house. As I looked at his blue eyes, his sensitive smile, I knew how difficult it would be for me to tell him about his parents. The evening passed pleasantly as we ate, made conversation, and listened to records. Then, as we were saying our good-byes, Dan asked if he could take me home. I agreed, happy to have his company. But at the same time, I knew that the painful truth could not remain hidden much longer. I took a deep breath as we walked downstairs.

Once outside, we started walking in the direction of Woodside. Dan began the conversation with the subject I had most wanted to avoid.

"I heard from Rose that you met my parents during the war. Will you tell me about them? I spent the last four years

Celia and Sala Landau, Hamburg, summer 1925.

Above: Photo postcard from Benno Landau (extreme right) with his brothers Max and Herman, Berlin, 1921. *Left:* Sala and Benno Landau, Hamburg, March 1922. *Facing page, top:* Celia (seated second from right) with her parents, Sala (center row, right) and Benno (last row, second from left), Haffkrug, 1929. *Near right:* Celia, Hamburg, 1929. *Far right:* Celia, first schoolday, Hamburg, spring 1931.

Celia and Karin, summer vacation in Bad Schwartau, 1933 (*left*), summer vacation in Duhnen, July 1935 (*below*).

Celia (*above*) and Karin (*right*), Hamburg, 1939.

Left: Crematorium, Bergen-Belsen, 1945. *Below:* Memorial plaque posted by the British army on the grounds of Bergen-Belsen. Photo taken by Celia Landau several weeks after liberation, May 1945. *Facing page, top:* Burned barracks area in Bergen-Belsen, August 1945. *Near right:* Celia in Bergen-Belsen, October 1945. *Far right:* Ohlsdorf cemetery, 1992. *Facing page, bottom:* Lucille Landau, New York City, summer 1946.

THE INFAMOUS BELSEN CONCENTRATION CAMP
Liberated by the British on 15 april 1945.

10,000 UNBURIED DEAD WERE FOUND HERE,
ANOTHER 13,000 HAVE SINCE DIED,
ALL OF THEM VICTIMS OF THE
GERMAN NEW ORDER IN EUROPE,
AND AN EXAMPLE OF NAZI KULTUR.

BENJAMIN LANDAU
GEB. 1. MAI 1893 – 5653
GEST. 31. JAN. 1941 – 5701

Left: Dan Eichengreen (U.S. Army), Casablanca, 1942. *Above:* Julie and Julius Eichengreen, Dan's parents, Hamburg, 1939. *Below:* Dan and Lucille Eichengreen, New York City, November 7, 1946.

as a soldier in the U.S. Army in Europe and tried to locate them, but without success. Are they alive?"

"From what I know, your parents are not alive." Without looking at him, I began to tell him about meeting his parents on the transport to the Lodz ghetto from Hamburg, how they had held hands, smiled, and remained patient. I told him how my friendship with Julie had developed during the first six weeks in the ghetto.

"We were housed in an empty, old, dirty school where we had to sleep on the cold, hard floor. Food was scarce. Mother, my sister Karin, and I were lucky to find a spot in the corner near the window. Your parents were next to us. On that first night, Mother and Karin, overcome by exhaustion, slept fitfully. I began crying, then sobbing. When your mother heard me, she slowly moved closer and put her arm around my shoulders. I was so grateful, and I felt very loving toward her."

Dan looked at me, sensing my pain and fatigue. "I see you are exhausted. Would you like to stop now?"

"I'm tired," I said, "but I'd rather get everything out of the way and over with."

"What did you think of my mother?" he asked.

I collected my courage and stamina and continued, "During those six weeks in the school, she and I were inseparable. We talked, we giggled; I admired her calm, patient disposition. Her hair was still red, intertwined with some gray. To me she was loving, gentle, and kind. She often talked of her only son who had left Germany for Cuba and would eventually come to New York."

"Yes, I left in the spring of 1939 for Cuba," Dan explained. "Since I entered basically with an illegal visa, the only work open to me and to those on my boat was farming. A young engineer, a doctor, and I rented a small farm, grew potatoes, corn, and bananas for a year and a half. It was hard work, but we had enough to eat and didn't mind. Conditions were primitive, and we lived an entirely different life than we had in years past. I heard from my parents regularly until the war broke out. Then the letters stopped." Dan sounded sad.

"But your mother never stopped talking about you! 'New York,' she would sigh with this dreamy, faraway look in her eyes, 'we'll be there, you and I,' she'd say, 'and you'll meet my son and together we'll walk along Broadway.' Then she would ask me to promise that if I got to New York before she did, I would look for you and tell you that they'd come as soon as possible. I promised."

I looked at Julie's son in the light of the street lamps. He kept on walking, his head lowered, staring at the pavement. I couldn't see his eyes.

"How did my parents look when you saw them last?"

"Thin and haggard. Only days after my last visit with them, on May 4, 1942, they were deported from the ghetto with thousands of others."

"Where to?"

"We weren't told. I waited for the postcard your mother had promised to send, but I never got it, and no one ever heard from anyone on that transport again. Later, much later, we learned that they had been sent to Chelmno. No one survived."

We had almost reached Woodside. I was drained and had nothing left to say.

"Thank you," Dan whispered.

"You are welcome is hardly the right response," I said sadly.

After a pause, Dan continued, "May I call you sometime? I would like to see you again—but not because you knew my parents."

I nodded.

The following week, Dan called. I was excited to hear from him and wondered what it would be like to see him when we didn't have to talk about the past. He had concert tickets and dinner reservations. Over dinner at the Russian Tea Room on Fifty-seventh Street, we talked about his job at a book distributor and about my job, which by now I hated; then we rushed off to Carnegie Hall. It was a wonderful concert! I had worn my new black silk dress and felt very elegant, as though I actually belonged in my surroundings. Life finally seemed to be taking a turn for the better.

The following week we went out for dinner again and then to the movies. By the middle of the next week, books, flowers, and candy began arriving. I happily anticipated Dan's calls; my spirit renewed, I felt a rebirth of excitement and enthusiasm for living.

We were seeing each other almost every weekend, and I knew I was falling in love. We went to concerts, to New York's marvelous museums, to the theater, and, when it was warm, to Jones Beach. Dan never seemed to run out of ideas. He was quiet, intelligent, and reliable, gentle and kind. Like me, he loved books, music, and politics. And I loved the yellow roses he sent. During the war there had been no flowers—only ashes.

Occasionally, I couldn't help but remember Szaja. Only now, after knowing Dan, did I understand just how selfish and unreliable Szaja had been. Dan was caring, loving, dependable, and unselfishly attentive to me. He took the time to understand me, to care about my feelings. He never again asked about the war. We enjoyed a mutual and trusting love.

He was planning a trip by train to California and suggested that I come with him. Perhaps we could see Uncle Adolf in San Francisco, then continue on to Los Angeles to meet Dan's cousins. I was reluctant to see the uncle who had refused to help his sister's family before the war. Nevertheless, I decided to make the trip.

By the time we left for California, we had known each other four months. On the first day of our trip, just after lunch, we were sitting in the lounge car taking in the passing scenery, and Dan was holding my hand. He suddenly turned, looked directly at me, and said, "I love you, will you marry me?"

Overwhelmed but not totally surprised, I answered, "Yes."

A few minutes later, Dan did surprise me. "I have saved this ring," he said. "It was my mother's. I would like you to have it."

I put the ring on my finger and immediately thought about Julie. Surely, she would have been happy for us.

We were married in New York on November 7, 1946, in the study of Rabbi Lieber with only a few friends and some of Dan's relatives in attendance. As I stood under the *khupe,* the rabbi's voice seemed to fade away. I was happy, yet I had also never been sadder or more painfully aware of the emptiness left by the loss of our families. I thought about my mother, my father, Karin, and Dan's parents. If only we could have received their blessings—if only they could have shared our joy. Why had the Nazis murdered them? Why?

Life together in the late forties was good for us. I had a wonderful husband, and our marriage was the basis for the normal life I had always wanted. With Dan's encouragement, I changed jobs. I also enrolled in evening school and studied typing, English, and history. Although we were not wealthy, we managed to go to the theater, concerts, and the opera. But just as the promise of a new life was beginning, ashes from the past would threaten to smother my hopes. My recurring nightmares continually invaded my sleep: the running, the flashlights, the fear. Dan would wake me and hold me, assuring me that it was only a nightmare. And I would feel secure again—but only till the next time.

My nightmares were not the only reminders of my past. One day in 1947 a letter from the Jewish community in Lodz arrived, a response to a letter I had written requesting information about Karin. The reply stated that she had been killed in 1942 with the other children in her transport from Lodz. Although this was confirmation of Karin's death, I still could not accept it as actual fact. Then I saw the signature at the bottom of the letter, "Director, Szaja Spiegel." I knew that Szaja must have investigated carefully before he'd sent this final, painful letter to me. I was devastated. Karin was really dead. Dan held me tightly. Neither one of us uttered a sound, but I knew that Dan shared the loss of my little sister with me.

In addition to the news of Karin's death, the first of many bills arrived from the Jewish community in Hamburg. They sent an accounting for the care and maintenance of my father's grave. I had mixed feelings. Whose ashes did the grave contain? Not my father's, for sure. "Ashes from Dachau," the Gestapo had said. Only after much soul-

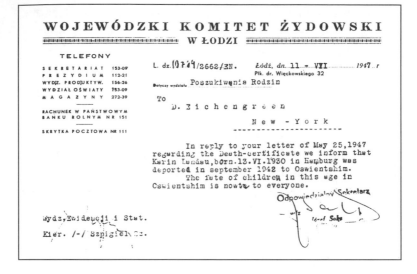

searching did I decide to pay the bill. Perhaps it didn't really matter whose ashes were buried beneath the stone that read, "Benjamin Landau."

Shortly after learning of Karin's death, I received yet another letter. Although it had a Hamburg postmark, the name on the outside of the envelope was not familiar. As far as I was concerned, anything from Germany was suspect. I opened the envelope slowly. Inside was a note from Wolfgang, the former SS guard at Neuengamme-Sasel. He reminded me of our bargain, my bribe to give him a house if he helped me escape from the camp. Now he wanted the house; the fact that he had not kept his end of the bargain was not mentioned. I pushed the letter across the table to Dan; he just shook his head. I furiously tore the letter into small pieces, put them into the ashtray, and set a match to them. Wolfgang, the coward, did not deserve a reply.

I wanted the past to go away, but the correspondence kept coming. I would have to learn to come to terms with it, but it wasn't going to be easy.

A letter came from Kommandant Stark's son. His father had been imprisoned with the other forty-one SS from Sasel Camp. Appealing to my decency and fairness, he asked for my help. His father wanted some positive statements about his character and background so that his son could obtain his release. I could only laugh as I remembered his father's decency and fairness: the beatings, our bruised and swollen faces, the kicking of our shins until they were black and blue. His abuse had been inhuman! This letter, too, ended in ashes.

Sofie, my coworker in the office at Sasel, wrote from Germany. She had been trained as a lawyer before the war. Now she was married, had a young son, and had decided to remain in Germany. She reminisced about how we had stolen food from the storage area adjacent to our office. Oberscharführer Pelz had carried the keys to the storage area on a string around his wrist, unless he went home on leave, which was about every three weeks. Then he would hide the keys in a drawer. He was meticulous in his administration, but we had noticed that whenever he went home on his day off, he would stuff the pockets of his coat with stolen food for his family. His habits and timing became quite predictable.

Sofie had acted as the lookout while I had stolen a few food items, never enough to be missed. Despite our fear, we had carried out the theft easily and had divided the spoils between us. We had devoured the food without tasting it or enjoying it, but we had at least relished the satisfaction of having outwitted the Germans for once.

My friend Elli wrote from Israel that she had married. Her health had improved after the removal of a lung, and she was expecting her first child. I was happy for her.

In this way, Dan slowly learned about my wartime friends, how our suffering had been made easier by our friendship, and how that friendship had contributed to our survival.

Szaja also wrote from Israel. He had left Poland in 1948 and was now finding life in Israel much easier. He was happily married to a schoolteacher and was continuing his life's work. He had published more than twenty books of poetry and prose about the ghetto—the pain, the hunger, the loves, and the losses. He sent copies for me to read. Occasionally, he would telephone, and we would talk about the ghetto years. Dan and I later made several trips to Israel, where we often spent time with Szaja and his wife. Our friendship continued until his death in June of 1990.

In February 1949, I was confronted with still another ghost from my past. One cold Saturday morning, Dan and I went to Altman's on Fifth Avenue so I could buy a pair of gloves. Dan decided to wait in the lobby. As I tried several pairs of gloves, my eyes were drawn to the large bony hands, long fingers, and brightly painted nails of the woman next to me. My gaze drifted upward to her face. She smiled. She had deep-set, dark brown eyes and a broad Slavic face with high cheekbones and a pointy chin. Her short black hair was combed stylishly into waves toward the back of her head. It was Maja—Auschwitz—1944! Maja the Kapo! My mind was flooded with images: shaven, ragged women; the barracks compound; watchtowers and electrified barbed wire. Maja had shouted orders, screamed threats, and beaten our bony backs at will with her gnarled stick. She had shown neither pity nor mercy.

"Maja! Auschwitz!" I blurted out.

Her smile disappeared, her face turned ashen. "How did you know?" she stammered.

My voice was scratchy as I replied, "I was there. You were part of the camp police, a Kapo. I never talked to you, but I'll never forget. It's you . . . your voice . . . your face . . ."

She looked stunned but did not deny it. "Oh, my God, what else do you remember about me?" She looked worried.

"I remember the stick, the beatings, and your screaming commands."

I could see her trembling. For one brief moment, the brash, cruel person I had known disappeared.

"I remember you were well fed. And there were rumors about an SS man who came to visit you at night in your private, privileged cubicle. He must have been the blond, tall one who returned during the day to beat us and laugh with sadistic pleasure at our suffering. We nicknamed him Siegfried." I had loathed Maja even more than the SS and had often wondered about the price she was paying to survive. But I could not condemn her for her will to live—what would I have done in her place?

Maja looked pleadingly at me and began to talk in a broken whisper, "Please give me a chance to explain . . ."

"What is there to explain?" I asked. I glanced once again at her hands. She wore a wedding band on her ring finger. "I see you are married," I said.

She nodded.

"Who is your husband?" I asked rudely.

She hesitated a long time before answering, "The German—he found me—after the war . . ."

"The former SS?" I asked incredulously.

She nodded again.

I was speechless. I watched her expressionless, pale face, and for a fleeting moment, I almost felt sorry for her. I might have been able to understand her behavior back then, but to marry a German SS—after the war—incomprehensible!

"Let me explain," Maja started again. "You are judging me by the past, and you have no right to do so. Circumstances were not normal then. I didn't care!" She sounded very angry and self-righteous. "Now I'm considered an outcast, a criminal by those who knew me then. There were others who were far worse than I during those years!

"Your memory is accurate," she went on, still angry and abrupt. "A nameless, faceless SS man came every night. I feared for my life and thought it would ensure my survival in Auschwitz. I loathed him then; I knew that he was a criminal and a killer. But as the months went by, I got used to him. He kept me out of the gas chamber. He gave me food. I didn't think of the future then. I lived one day at a time. Whatever I did was my way of surviving."

She paused, and then, with great effort, she continued. "After the war I spent two years in Germany in a displaced persons' camp. He found me there, but I refused to see him or to talk to him. Then I came to New York. He followed me again. He kept coming back into my life. I knew his past, and he knew mine. I was tired of running and hiding. We decided to start a new life together. Can you understand? I didn't do anything wrong!"

I didn't want to judge her, but I couldn't help myself. "Do you have children?"

Again, she hesitated a long time. "No, not yet, maybe in a few years . . ."

"And you can think of having his children? He was a war criminal—is still a war criminal—and you are part of the betrayal of all human life and decency!"

Although I actually could have denounced her, I knew I would not. But for the first time, her eyes filled with fear; she, too, knew that I could report both of them to the American authorities. Perhaps more importantly, I was not telling her what she wanted to hear—that I understood, that I forgave her, that she had done nothing wrong. Unable to speak, I simply shook my head. I had to get away, not from this fearful, weeping woman, but from the Kapo, Maja, and the hideous past we shared. I ran to the lobby and fell sobbing into Dan's arms.

In 1949, Dan and I accepted jobs in San Francisco. No one there knew about me or my past, and no one asked about it. I preferred it that way. Although the nightmares continued, I resigned myself to their ongoing presence. The climate, the palm trees, our new jobs, new car, and new house brought me a greater sense of security and hope. Gradually, the intrusions from the past diminished in intensity and number and began to recede in the rush of my happiness and the bustle of my new life. Perhaps I had finally come home.

Our two sons were born in 1952 and 1956, and I, who once had not wanted to bring new life into such a degenerate world, found much joy in the arrival of these two small souls. Dan and I felt great satisfaction when they, as Jews, continued their ancient, rich heritage. We gave them the Hebrew names of their murdered grandfathers: Benjamin and Mosche.

Fifty Years Later... ~

1991

The invitation from the city government of Hamburg, signed by its mayor, Dr. Vorscherau, came unexpectedly. I had been identified in a photo from the exhibit "Jüdisches Leben am Grindel" (Jewish Life at the Grindel) on display at the Historical Museum in 1990. Both my maiden name and my married name had been prominently displayed and had resulted in this official invitation to spend six days in Hamburg as the city's guest. The scheduled events included an official reception at the Rathaus (city hall), with a luncheon set for two days after our arrival.

Deciding whether to accept the invitation was not easy. I had intended never to return to either Germany or Poland. Several times previously, Dan and I had made reservations, only to cancel them later. On each occasion, the reasons were the same: too many emotions, too many memories—all of them painful. The Nazis' attempt to exterminate European Jewry had been centered in the camps located on German and Polish soil. The people of those countries had been either active participants or silent witnesses, and although I do not subscribe completely to the notion of "collective

194 ~ From Ashes to Life

guilt," surely each of us must take responsibility for his or her own individual actions. Not a single German or Pole had offered me help when I had needed it. Moreover, it had been nearly fifty years since I left Germany and Poland, and now no one lived there whom I could call or contact—no friends from the past, no neighbors, not even any of my father's former business associates.

Dan and I considered all the circumstances carefully. There were lots of reasons to be apprehensive, but we also reasoned that this was 1991 and that surely things had changed. In any case, once there, we could leave any time we so desired. In the end, it was our need to know that tipped the balance, for we had many unanswered questions: had the Germans and Poles changed in their attitude toward Jews? Had they experienced some remorse, some regrets? What was the present state of Jewish life and culture in Germany and Poland? Were any of the buildings we had known as children still standing?

I also wanted to satisfy a personal need: to visit the graves of my parents. Visiting the graves meant reexperiencing and reexamining two dilemmas that I had as yet been unwilling and unable to resolve. First, would I ever be able to make peace with the fact that my parents had been senselessly murdered—would it ever be understandable? Second, I knew that the ashes buried beneath the stone that read "Benjamin Landau" were not those of my father and that my mother's grave with the wooden marker that Karin and I had made would be long gone. If I visited these "graves," how could I possibly find the spiritual closeness that one hopes for at the grave of a loved one? But then again, I had nothing else. So, finally, we accepted the invitation and decided that we would go first to Hamburg and then on to Poland.

The Lufthansa flight was smooth and uneventful, but at the airport in Hamburg, the first sign, "Fuhlsbüttel," the name of the district where the airport is located, brought back bitter memories. A large concentration camp had been located there. Dan had spent time within its walls in 1933 and again in 1937, as had my father in 1939. Jews had been confined there and treated worse than criminals. Their only crime: born Jewish.

The taxi drove us toward the downtown area. We passed Gärtnerstrasse, the street where my father and my uncle had owned an apartment house at number 57. It was still standing. We were dropped off at the Hotel Basel, which overlooked the Alster, a beautiful lake within the city. The accommodations were adequate, but the personnel behind the front desk were barely polite. I guessed that they had been informed of the arrival of Jews from abroad. I felt ill at ease as I looked at the Germans. The ones my age or older looked well fed, sensibly dressed, and sounded loud and arrogant, just as they had before the war. I was aware that I was being critical, but how could I be objective? Almost fifty years later, I couldn't stop looking over my shoulder for someone from my past—a guard from one of the camps, perhaps, or our neighbor, Brinkschneider, a member of the SA.

Two days later, at noon, Dan and I attended the official reception at the Rathaus. The building was still magnificent. In the plaza in front of it stood a statue of Heinrich Heine, the Jewish poet. The statue had been erected after the war, but I remembered that during my school years, by official German policy, Heine's name had been omitted from all his poems. Instead, at the end of each poem, it had read, "Dichter Unbekannt" (poet unknown).

The reception hall was crowded. We had learned that the invitations from the mayor's office were being sent periodically, as a goodwill gesture, to small groups of Jews who had been forced to flee Hamburg and had never returned. However, there were only about twenty Jewish people from around the world who had returned for this visit. Most of them were in their eighties or older, and only a few were still in their sixties. Some of them had come, like us, to gather information; others had come for sentimental reasons. For me, there was nothing sentimental about the past.

At the far side of the large hall was a crowd of German officials, schoolteachers, researchers, and others who had been asked to attend. None of them came over to introduce themselves or to welcome their Jewish guests.

The luncheon included a long welcoming speech from one of the city officials. He made no reference to the recent history of either the Jews or the Germans. His speech was cordial but mentioned no regrets. There was no promise that the persecution of Jews or any other human beings would not happen again or that the Germans would not allow history to be repeated.

We met a young couple, Ursula and Wil, both of them historians, and an old schoolmate of Dan's who had returned from England to live in Germany. Had it not been for them, I don't think I would have been able to stay the two hours. Although perfectly "proper," the reception was cold and impersonal, perhaps an empty gesture made for public relations. Dan and I left feeling like the outsiders we were.

The following day, Dan and I visited the synagogue that had been built after the war as a replacement for the great synagogue that had stood on Bornplatz. The old synagogue had been burned and vandalized on Kristallnacht, November 9, 1938. Its replacement stood in an entirely different neighborhood, on Hohe Weide, and was surrounded by a high metal fence. There was a bell and speaker system at the entrance, so it was impossible to enter unless the visit had been arranged ahead of time. After much ringing, knocking, and rattling of the gate, someone finally came and agreed to let us in—but only after checking our identification! Why was it so difficult to visit a Jewish synagogue in Hamburg in 1991?

I asked the business manager why this place of worship was so securely guarded and why it had not been rebuilt on the old site at Bornplatz. His answers were short and to the point: the security measures were to prevent Arab terrorist attacks and antisemitic vandalism. They had not rebuilt on Bornplatz because it would have been too close to the University of Hamburg. I didn't understand what the proximity of the university had to do with the synagogue. Was he implying that they were worried about antisemitic attacks from students? When I looked at him uncomprehendingly, he repeated, "Fear of antisemitism and its consequences." I was speechless. Young university students—a possible threat?

I was shocked and saddened to learn that the Jews of Hamburg were apparently still afraid of antisemitic incidents. They were still worried about drawing attention to themselves, still being looked upon as outsiders, still being abused. I had hoped that the lessons of fifty years ago would have brought change. I had expected an open acceptance of Jewish culture and religious practices. Instead, I encountered a double disappointment: many Germans, young as well as old, continued to demonstrate antisemitic ugliness. And the even greater disappointment was that the Jews still played by the Germans' rules, sacrificing in the process their dignity and self-respect as human beings. Hadn't they learned from the Israelis that they had to fight back when attacked? Hadn't they heard of due process in the courts?

We left the synagogue and walked toward Hohe Weide 25 where my family had lived from 1928 to 1937, before being forced to live in "Jewish buildings." The condominium still stood. It looked somewhat older but was still well maintained. The curtains at the second-floor windows, where our dining room and living room had been, were white and lacy, very different from the ones my parents had used. Dan asked me if I wanted to go upstairs, but I had only one desire: to leave.

We had buried my father in February 1941. More correctly, we had buried a little cigar box filled with "ashes from Dachau" in the Jewish cemetery in Ohlsdorf. I had never gone back. Throughout these many years, I had felt delinquent. Jewish custom dictates regular visits before specific holy days, but I had been unwilling to come face to face with this grave or with the pain and anger it evoked. It had taken me fifty years to confront this place, and I knew that I would never return again.

The gray stone marker that read "Benjamin Landau" was worn. Pale letters spelled out my father's name and the dates of his birth and death. I broke down and cried. I wondered if I should recite the Kaddish, the Hebrew prayer for the dead. Its words glorify God and his mercy, but after Auschwitz, I had stopped believing in either one. Nevertheless, I said the prayer, if only to show respect for my slain father. Afterward, as is Jewish custom, I left small pebbles on top of the gravestone.

I would never be sure that this was really my father's grave. And though I tried to convince myself that this didn't really matter, I knew it did. On the way back to the subway, we passed a masonry shop. On impulse, I walked in, asked if they did repair work, and ordered the stone cleaned, the letters blackened. I paid for the work and asked them to send me a photo when they had completed it. Since there was a gravestone, at least the letters ought to be readable.

Shortly before we left Germany, we got to spend more time with Wil and Ursula. They asked a lot of questions, questions they had asked of their parents but for which they had never received satisfactory answers. How could the Holocaust have happened? Why had there been so little resistance on the part of the Jews? Why had so few Germans helped the Jews? These questions had caused controversy and enmity within their own families. They had carefully researched and studied the German past, yet for them, as for most of the rest of the world, Hitler's initiation of the Holocaust and the subsequent conformity or apathy of most of the German people about his plan for genocide were difficult, if not impossible, to understand or forgive. They looked at us, survivors of the Holocaust, with sadness and compassion.

It was time to leave Germany. Although I did not regret coming, I was not sorry to go. But I wondered what we would find in Poland.

As the Swissair jet came to a stop on the Warsaw runway, announcements were made in German, French, and Polish.

Looking out the window, I became acutely aware that I was back in the country of Auschwitz, Treblinka, and the ghettos. This country had once been the home of my parents, my grandparents, and their parents before them.

Our friends from St. Paul, Minnesota, Leon and Felicia Weingarten, who had met us in Zurich and traveled with us to Poland, had also once called Poland their home. That was before the onset of World War II in 1939. But even in the 1920s and 1930s, the Poles had not been known for their fondness of Jews. It was, in fact, antisemitism that had motivated my parents to leave Poland and settle in Germany—"a more civilized, progressive country," my father used to say. How wrong he had been!

I still cherished the memories of summer vacations at my grandmother's house in Sambor. But any memories beyond those were unthinkable and unspeakable. I had just turned sixteen when I was shipped, like merchandise, to the Lodz ghetto. My years in the ghetto and at Auschwitz had been filled with treachery, fear, hunger, and suffering and had driven me to the brink of insanity. My feelings had been deadened. I had lost my mother and sister here; I alone had survived to struggle with the burden of guilt and despair.

As the doors of the plane were opened, I again felt numb. My hands were clammy, and I could feel my heart racing. I was filled with trepidation. The road to the past had begun in Germany and would end—somehow—in Poland.

The air was humid, and a soft drizzle, like tears, fell as we traveled by taxi on little-used highways and streets to our hotel, the Novotel. We dropped off our bags, then hailed another taxi and asked the driver to take us to the area of the former Warsaw ghetto. We drove through the old streets, but none of the Warsaw ghetto buildings were still standing; all had been destroyed by the Germans in carrying out Hitler's "scorched-earth" policy. Now the rebuilt neighborhood consisted mainly of apartment buildings. We surmised that not too many Jews occupied them.

On a quiet street, adjacent to a small, ill-kept park, was an impressive bronze memorial commemorating the Warsaw ghetto uprising of 1943. The large monument, designed by Nathan Rapoport, depicts the ghetto fighters on one side and the huddled, stooped figures of martyrs on the other. In the background, barely noticeable, there are three Nazi helmets and two bayonets. Its inscription, in Polish, Yiddish, and Hebrew, is addressed to the fallen Jews. The area around the memorial had been neglected, and we noticed that it was often used as a dog walk. This memorial seemed to me to have been merely a perfunctory gesture.

A ten-minute drive away, close to the former ghetto, there was another "memorial," a black and white stone wall with a gate marked "Umschlagplatz." This was where the Germans had assembled Jews, loaded them onto trucks and trains, and sent them to their deaths. There was neither a plaque nor an explanation of what had taken place here.

We asked the driver to take us to the Warsaw synagogue. Its entrance was on a side street and would have been impossible for us to find without a guide. I wondered if this synagogue, like the one in Hamburg, was unmarked for its own protection. The synagogue was small, lovely, and traditional in its furnishings. I admired the sanctuary, its high ceiling, the wooden benches on either side separating the men from the women, and the satin curtain in front of the cabinet that housed the Torah. Although the building had been used as a stable during the German occupation, it was once again a sanctuary for Warsaw's remaining Jews. Before 1939, there had been three and a half million Jews living in Poland; we were told that now there were no more than five thousand. A culture and a people that had existed for hundreds of years—almost extinct. The Third Reich had accomplished that. I could feel only fury and disgust.

In the sanctuary, we were greeted by an old, crippled man, who told us, "We have no weddings, no births, and no Brith Milahs [rites of circumcision]. There are only old people left. The young ones emigrated long ago to Israel and America. In a few years, when my generation is gone, this building and the monuments will be all that's left of a once-flourishing community and culture. This is the end of the line."

His words sank in slowly. The realization was heartbreaking. It was still difficult to believe that one man's inhumane, fanatic vision had almost extinguished an entire people and their culture. Of the eleven million Jews in Europe, 55 percent had been exterminated in twelve years.

The Jewish Museum, on a small street nearby, was dark; only a few paintings, some silver artifacts, and other remembrances of a once-rich cultural heritage remained. It seemed beyond all human understanding. My heart filled with anguish at the thought of the loss, the suffering that my people had endured.

The taxi driver was watching us. He did not seem compassionate or understanding. I wondered if he was even old enough to know about what had happened to the Jews in Poland. But I had the distinct feeling that even had he known, such knowledge would not have aroused his compassion or sympathy. We encountered similar attitudes over the next few days, as we talked to people in stores, in the hotel, in restaurants, and in taxis. No mention was ever made of the past, of the Jews who had called this place home and were now gone—forever.

On Sunday we hired a driver and car for the trip to Lodz. I had spent more than three years in the "Balut," the slum district of Lodz, during the German occupation. The horrible memories of those years came flooding back during the ride: my mother's starvation, Karin's deportation . . . I felt both anticipation and dread as we drove on.

The highways were almost deserted. The farmhouses we passed were neat and clean and looked much more prosperous than the buildings in Warsaw. The prosperity was belied, however, by the plows and wagons pulled by old scraggly horses.

We entered Lodz at the center of the former ghetto: Balucki Rynek. Now the square was just a grassy area and seemed cheerful and harmless. My vision of this place, however, was colored by the events of another life. In 1941, there had been barracks that had housed the headquarters of the ghetto administration, both Jewish and German. Rumkowski, "Der Ältester der Juden" of the ghetto, had run his kingdom from this exact place. He had agreed to, and helped carry out, the commands of the Germans, accepting and executing the deportation orders. In the end, he himself had been deported, and as soon as he had arrived in Auschwitz, the Germans had killed him. There had been no special privileges—not even for the king of the ghetto. To the Germans, Rumkowski had been merely another expendable Jew.

We continued to Plac Koscielny 4, opposite an old church. This was where I had worked for the director of archives of the Statistical Department, Dr. Oskar Singer. The building was dilapidated and looked very different than I remembered it, much smaller and narrower. But once I was inside, everything looked the same. The walls were a dirty yellow, the doors brown, and the stairways filthy, just like fifty years ago. Here we had kept a chronicle of the daily lives of the ghetto dwellers: their hospitalizations, their deportations, deaths, suffering, pain, allotted food rations, and the hunger —always the hunger. Dr. Singer had hoped that perhaps after the war there would at least be records to tell the world the truth about the horrors of our dismal existence. His hope was realized; after the war, the chronicles were found. They were edited by Dr. Lucjan Dobroszycki and published in 1984 under the title, *The Chronicle of the Lodz Ghetto*. For Dr. Singer himself, however, Auschwitz had been the final stop.

Diagonally across the street was the little red-brick house with the white trim and the black iron fence around it— the Kripo, short for Kriminalpolizei. It looked totally unchanged, except that it now appeared innocent and peaceful. But I could still feel the German's fist on my face and taste the blood on my tongue. And I still suffered the consequences, a dull deafness in my left ear. The damage had been permanent.

We drove on to Lutomierska Street where the Department of Labor had been housed. It was now just a plain, run-down building. Its director, Leonard Luft, had survived, become prosperous, and lived under a different name on the East Coast of the United States. At the very end of a recent television presentation of the film *The Lodz Ghetto,* Leonard Luft had been introduced as Bernard Fleming, the only surviving member of the ghetto administration. During the war, he had supposedly supplied deportation lists and followed other German orders that increased the hardships of his fellow Jews. But for his TV interview, he repeatedly stressed that he had nothing to hide and nothing to be ashamed of. Still, I remembered my many discouraging visits to his office and Luft's threats of having me physically removed if I once again requested work.

We soon arrived at Rybna 8, the office building where I had met, worked with, and fallen in love with Szaja Spiegel. Here, during the daytime, we had completed millions of coal ration forms for the German population in the Reich. At noon, we would receive our meager ration of soup. And here, too, after work and late into the evening, Szaja would read his poetry and prose to me and then ask for my response.

These offices had now been converted into apartments. The three-story edifice that I remembered had been fairly new, freshly painted, and much more spacious than the actual ruin in front of me. Across the street, the post office still stood. From here, I had mailed the two postcards that we were permitted to send out of the ghetto.

Around the corner was Pawia 24, where I had lived with my mother and sister for almost a year. It was unchanged. The old, three-story building was shabby, its walls cracked and peeling. It was as if time had stood still. Only the barbed wire and the guardhouse had disappeared. Behind the building, the outhouses were still in use! The bakery across the street was still selling goods. In 1942, we could only watch hungrily through the barbed wire while the Poles carried home their warm bread.

I looked up at the small window on the second floor, the

window that had offered only a little light and air to the room where I had watched my mother die of starvation. In the very same yard below, my little sister had been "selected" by the Germans to be murdered. It was deserted now and quiet, but I could still hear Karin's pleading cries and see her hands stretching out to me as I stood there, impotent and paralyzed.

Not much had changed in fifty years. The pump by the front door had disappeared, and the individual rooms had been converted into three- and four-room apartments. In the little side yard, covered by high grass, I found the wooden cover of the dry well where Szaja and I had talked, embraced, and kissed.

We went on to Bazarny Rynek. The square was paved with cobblestones interspersed with grassy squares, and it looked almost lovely. But in my mind's eye, I could still see the gallows neatly placed around the square and the bodies of the hanged men swaying in the breeze—the Germans' warning to those who might disobey orders.

When we stopped opposite Mlynarska 25, I told Dan that this was where the Germans had housed the deportees from Hamburg; Dan's parents, my mother, Karin, and I had lived here during our first six weeks in the ghetto, crowded body to body, Julie and Julius sleeping next to us on the floor. The building was abandoned now. Farther on, we found the building on Zgierska Street where Julie and Julius had lived for just a few short months before they had been deported and had disappeared forever.

The memories engulfed and, finally, overwhelmed me. The sobbing was more than Dan could bear, and he wanted to leave. I, too, was eager to get away, but the past would not let me go. I had not dreamed this nightmare. I had lived it. I had known every nook and cranny of this place. Yet even as I stood on these same ghetto streets, it seemed impossible that this had been my reality.

We had been given the address of the Jewish Community House in Lodz where I hoped to get some information that would help me locate my mother's grave. We had trouble finding the building; although we had the correct street and number, there was no sign that indicated a Jewish agency. Only after we drove into the courtyard did we see, over the narrow archway, the white metal plate directing us to the second floor.

As we climbed the stairs, we were shocked by the filth around us. We walked down a dark hallway that led into a small office where two elderly men sat at their desks. The room was barren and pitiful, in a state of decay.

I began in Yiddish, "Shalom. Could you please help us with information about a grave location?"

The two men smiled. The younger one, about seventy years old, was tall and gaunt. His shirt was too large for his thin neck. "So you have come from America, the land of millionaires!" he said. "Well, give me the name of the dead and the date of death."

"Sala Landau, July 13, 1942," I replied.

From behind the desk, he pulled out long, narrow boxes filled with thousands of file cards that went back more than seventy years.

"Landau, Sara, Sala, Landau, Landau ..." He checked and rechecked. No card was to be found.

"In 1942, few records were kept," the tall man said.

"There were too many ghetto deaths, and staying alive was more important than keeping records of the dead. Sorry."

"I was there, I remember," I said.

He looked at me. "Really?" There was disbelief in his voice.

The older of the two, poorly but cleanly dressed and probably in his midseventies, was quiet, but his head kept turning toward our voices. He didn't get up. He was blind. I couldn't help wondering why these two were still in Poland, living this dismal, pitiful existence. We thanked them, pressed a bill into their hands, and left for the cemetery, determined to locate the grave despite the lack of records or directions.

We drove along a narrow, cobblestoned street. On our right, we saw a long, red-brick wall that looked familiar. I remembered that it surrounded the huge cemetery, but during the ghetto days, we had entered from the opposite side where there was a huge open space. We found a small, iron door in the wall. It was unlocked, so we walked in. In front of us was the brick building with the large Magen David exactly as I remembered it from 1942. During the war, the ghetto dead had been piled high against the inside walls of this building. The smell... Karin and I searching for Mother's decaying body... the name tag tied to her ankle... Now the empty room reverberated for me with the silent anguish of those years.

We left quickly and proceeded with our search. Just in front of the iron gate that led to the grave sites was a large, granite slab resembling an oversized headstone. Its Yiddish inscription memorializes the ghetto dead and numbers them at sixty thousand. When we entered the cemetery, we noticed gravestones that were a hundred years old, some partially destroyed, others broken. Time and neglect had done much damage.

A tall, skinny figure wearing a long, coatlike garment, a worn cap, and shabby boots had been quietly watching us. His black, stringy hair stuck out of his cap, and he smiled through his few remaining teeth. Hardly more than forty-five years old, he looked grotesque. He approached us and, speaking in Yiddish, Polish, and English, told us that his name was Jakub. He explained that the cemetery had a non-Jewish caretaker and that he helped out only occasionally. He pointed to a huge, uneven, hilly area covered with weeds and wild, grassy plants. "The ghetto dead," he said, "have hardly any gravestones. We have no names, no grave numbers, and cannot identify them."

Now and then a stone tablet showed a name, but there were hardly a dozen of these. All the other graves were indistinguishable from each other. A large green carpet covered the nameless ghetto murdered. I stood silently and looked around, remembering how Karin and I, under the hot July sun, had dug Mother's small grave near a walkway in the cemetery. Neither of us had said a word or shed a tear. Now, in the same place, fifty years later, the wind gently brushed through the high grass. I looked around for a quiet place, and then, as I had for my father, I recited the Kaddish. The tears that had not come in 1942 were streaming down my cheeks. Many minutes passed before I slowly began walking toward the gates. I knew I would never return.

From what seemed like a great distance, I heard someone say, "Shalom." An elderly couple was lovingly watering the green shrubs on a grave. The large, impressive stone had obviously been set there a long time ago, and I assumed that it belonged to their parents or perhaps even to their grand-parents. I responded but continued walking, lost in my sor-row, toward the small iron door in the brick wall that led to the street.

Again I heard, "Shalom." They had followed me. I turned and for the first time really noticed them. He was short and thin, and his face looked worn, tired, and very old. I was struck by his large, beaked nose. He wore a long, khaki-colored army overcoat and a matching cap. She was small and a little plump. Her white, wavy hair framed a kind, wrinkled face. On her lips was a touch of lipstick. Her gray coat was threadbare but very clean. Both of them must have been in their eighties.

"Why have you come? What are you doing here?" The words rushed out of the man's mouth.

"My mother's grave...I buried her in 1942...the ghetto," I began.

They looked at me. "You can't have been in the ghetto—it's too long ago!"

I nodded. "I came here when I was barely sixteen. And you?" I asked.

"I fought in the Polish army and later with the partisans. I returned after the war and stayed. I practiced law until recently."

The woman had taken my hand and continued to hold it tightly. "I was in hiding with Aryan papers," she added.

"Your name?" I asked.

"It was Gold," he answered, "but to avoid problems, we changed our name to Dembiak."

"Problems, after the war?" I asked.

They nodded.

"Antisemitism?"

They nodded again.

"And still you stayed in Poland?"

They smiled sadly and shrugged their shoulders. I felt such compassion for these two elderly people; it was as if I had known them all my life. They didn't want the cigarettes we offered, and only after much pleading did the woman accept lipstick and stockings. They were obviously poor but very proud. We exchanged addresses, promising to write and help them if at all possible. We embraced, we cried, and then Dan and I parted from our newfound friends. This was what remained of our people in Poland; in a few years, even they would be gone.

The next day my friend Felicia insisted that we go to Auschwitz. Both she and I had spent time there in 1944.

"It's near Kraków, and I have to return just one time," she said.

"I have no desire to go back," I said. "Auschwitz is the last place I ever want to see again." The horrors, the chimneys, and the smell of the smoke had remained with me these past fifty years; I had no need to refresh those memories. A few days later, however, I gave in to Felicia's insistence.

The drive was long and tiresome. On the way, we stopped in Kraków. My parents had taken me there in 1930, and I recalled every detail: our laughter, how we ran around the town square, the impressive cathedral, the old synagogue, the yeshiva, and even the market halls. Neither time nor war had changed this place, but both had brought about changes in the population. Now there were only a handful of Jews, all old and broken souls. Here, too, the last traces of Judaism were disappearing, becoming history—relegated only to words on paper.

Auschwitz was only a short ride away. As we approached the site of the former camp, I was struck by the absence of any significant monument or detailed description of this place. There was no mention of the number of Jews killed here, barely any reference to Jews at all. A placard stated that Poles and people of other nationalities had perished here, but it did not mention that the majority of them were Jews.

The permanent buildings, which had been used to house long-term inmates, were now set up as museums. Echoes of the past cried out. Thousands of human beings had been slaughtered here, sent to their deaths by gassing, but the hundreds of Polish schoolchildren who had come for a "visit" on this day seemed to know little of the actual history of this place. They laughed and chatted and did not seem the least bit affected by what they saw. Perhaps it was not surprising. The unspeakable, inhuman cruelties and the once-screaming, now-silent voices of despair, bewilderment, and fear had been compressed into only a few photographs and some sparsely worded descriptions.

We got back into the car and drove on to Auschwitz-Birkenau, a sprawling area still crowded with the original barracks that used to house us. Row after row seemed to sprout out of the ground, still surrounded by barbed wire. Even the railroad tracks leading from the countryside through the iron gate to the narrow platform inside were still there. My throat was tight, and I had difficulty swallowing. I felt paralyzed; I could not enter the camp compound. I felt total contempt for all the Germans who had instigated and carried out this diabolical plot to eliminate European Jewry. The horror and fear of long ago took hold of me again. We started the car and left; I did not look back.

We had undertaken the journey to Germany and Poland seeking information about the past as well as the present. I brought with me unanswered questions about the Holocaust, as well as hopes and expectations for the present state of Jewish culture and traditions in these countries. I had hoped to find some remorse—or at least some respectful remembrance—on the part of those who had inflicted the horrors of the Holocaust on the Jews. I had also hoped that the lessons of the past might have resulted in a greater acceptance of Jewish cultural and religious practices. I had expected to find freedom, respect, and human dignity accorded to all citizens equally. Finally, I had hoped to find the courage to visit the graves of my parents. Only this last hope was realized. All of the other hopes and expectations were almost completely dispelled.

Although the antisemitism we encountered was not as extensive or intense as that which we had experienced fifty years earlier, it still found insidious forms of expression. Moreover, the Jews in Germany were, once again, accepting the status of citizens with second-class privileges. Instead of finding remorse—silence. Instead of receiving sincere remembrances and respect—perfunctory gestures. Instead of witnessing acceptance—covert disregard. My questions regarding the current vitality of Jewish cultural life in both Germany and Poland were answered. And in spite of the preparation that my knowledge of the past might have given me, the answers were devastating! The reality of the extent of the loss of Jewish people and their cultural practices came as a stunning shock from which I can hardly expect to recover.

How is it possible that some people can actually question the occurrence of the Holocaust, question the extent of the anguish, the suffering, and the numbers maimed and murdered? Ironically, the Germans themselves provide the evidence that dispels such questions. As I discovered in the process of writing this book, the German government maintains carefully detailed, blatantly revealing records of the names, places, deportations, transports, and transport numbers, as well as the dates of the deaths and burials, of those same human beings whom it strove—with such a vengeance—to eliminate from the face of the earth.

The question that remains unanswered but that must continue to be asked for the sake of all humankind is how to understand the Nazis' holy reverence for documentation—and their holy irreverence for the lives of those human beings they selected for the "Endlösung"—the "Final Solution."

About Lucille Eichengreen ～

Photo: Ed Kirwan Graphic Arts

Lucille Eichengreen was born Cecilia Landau in Hamburg, Germany, in 1925. A survivor of the Lodz ghetto and Auschwitz, Neuengamme, and Bergen-Belsen concentration camps, she fled to Paris in 1945 and then, in 1946, made her way to New York, where she met her future husband, Dan Eichengreen. In the following years, she worked as an insurance agent while she finished her education. In 1949, Eichengreen moved with her husband to Berkeley, California, where their sons, Barry and Martin, were born. Now retired, she writes and speaks on the Holocaust at schools, colleges, and universities.